THE
KOREAN
KITCHEN

THE KOREAN KITCHEN: 75 HEALTHY, DELICIOUS and EASY RECIPES

Copyright © 2014 by Korean Food Promotion Institute
Project Planning by Dong Hee Kim, Mi Sook Kim, Mee Hwa Song (KFPI)
Project Director by Lana Chung (Kyung Hee University)
Food&Food Text by Boksun Han (Han Boksun Food Culture Research Institute)
Editorial Supervision by Gloryvee Ramos (University of Houston), James Robert Nasella (Ottens Flavors)
English Editing by Jiseon Kim

All rights reserved.

First published in 2014
Revised edition, 2018
Third printing, 2023
by Hollym International Corp., Carlsbad, CA, USA
Phone 760 814 9880
http://www.hollym.com   **e-Mail** contact@hollym.com

Hollym

Published simultaneously in Korea
by Hollym Corp., Publishers, Seoul, Korea
Phone +82 2 734 5087   **Fax** +82 2 730 5149
http://www.hollym.net   **e-Mail** hollym@hollym.co.kr

ISBN: 978-1-56591-459-9
Library of Congress Control Number: 2014955765

Printed in Korea

THE KOREAN KITCHEN

75 HEALTHY, DELICIOUS and EASY RECIPES

by Korean Food Promotion Institute

Hollym
Carlsbad, CA and Seoul

PROLOGUE

Food culture is a representative medium that informs national identity and culture, and it is a valuable asset for increasing the national brand value.

Even if we do not know our language or history, we can quickly become acquainted through food culture. This is the reason why food culture has always been at the top of the global communication index released each year.

To enjoy Korean food culture with other citizens of the world, the Korean Food Promotion Institute has attempted to investigate various resources on Korean food and to inform others about the value of modernized Korean cuisine.

South Korea participated as the guest of honor in the "Madrid Fusion" conference on fermented food that was held in 2012, and the history and culture of Korean food received considerable attention.

Moreover, "Korean kimchi and kimchi culture" was listed as a UNESCO world intangible cultural heritage last December; thus, Korean food culture is not only a Korean resource but also a worldwide cultural asset that should be preserved and passed on.

Global curiosity and interest in Korean food has increased since Korean food was listed by UNESCO. Therefore, the Korean Food Promotion Institute published a Korean cookbook to allow the citizens of the world to cook Korean food with ease.

"The Korean Kitchen : 75 Healthy and Delicious Recipes" was released to introduce representative Korean traditional dishes that are preferred by Americans.

I hope that "Korean Food for the World" becomes a friend to the global kitchen, and I hope it is absorbed into everyday cooking and not just used for special meals.

I deeply appreciate the hard work of the cookbook's authors, and I hope that families around the world will be encouraged to eat bulgogi and kimchi at home.

2014
Chairperson of the Korean Food Promotion Institute

CONTENTS

04   PROLOGUE

Korean Cuisine Culture

- 08   Nature's Influence on Korean Cuisine
- 10   Characteristics of Korean Cuisine

Ingredients and Basic Techniques of Korean Cuisine

- 14   Basic Ingredients of Korean Cuisine
- 32   Shopping for Korean Ingredients in Other Countries
- 36   Essential Ingredients for Korean Cuisine
- 36   Essential Korean Kitchenware
- 37   Converting Measurements
- 38   Basic Techniques

Top 12 Korean Food

- 52   Bibimbap Rice Mixed with Vegetables and Beef
- 54   Sundubu-jjigae Spicy Soft Dubu Stew
- 56   Mandu Dumplings
- 58   Bulgogi Grilled Marinated Beef
- 60   Galbi-jjim Braised Short Ribs in Soy Sauce
- 62   Dwaeji-bulgogi (Jeyuk-bokkeum) Spicy Stir-fried Pork
- 64   Modum-jeon Assorted Savory Pancakes
- 66   Haemul-pajeon Seafood and Green Onion Pancake
- 68   Japchae Stir-fried Sweet Potato Noodles and Vegetables
- 70   Gimbap Toasted Laver Rolls
- 72   Tteok-bokki Stir-fried Rice Cakes with Gochu-jang Sauce
- 74   Maekom-dak-gangjeong Deep-fried Chicken with Sweet and Spicy Sauce

Rice, Porridge and Noodles

- 78 Huin-bap · Ogok-bap Cooked White Rice · Cooked Five-grain Rice
- 80 Kimchi-bokkeum-bap Kimchi Fried Rice
- 82 Hobak-juk Pumpkin Porridge
- 84 Patjuk Red Bean Porridge
- 86 Mul-naengmyeon Buckwheat Noodles in Chilled Broth
- 88 Bibim-naengmyeon Spicy Buckwheat Noodles
- 90 Janchi-guksu (On-myeon) Noodles in Anchovy Broth
- 92 Goldong-myeon (Bibim-guksu) Noodles Mixed with Vegetables and Beef
- 94 Kal-guksu Noodles in Broth
- 96 Tteokguk Sliced Rice Cake Soup

Soups and Stews

- 100 Miyeok-guk Seaweed Soup
- 102 Sigeumchi-doenjang-guk Spinach Soybean Paste Soup
- 104 Oi-naengguk Chilled Cucumber Soup
- 106 Doenjang-jjigae Soybean Paste Stew
- 108 Kimchi-jjigae Kimchi Stew
- 110 So-gogi-beoseot-jeongol Beef and Mushroom Hot Pot
- 112 Yukgaejang Spicy Beef Soup
- 114 Samgye-tang Ginseng Chicken Soup

Special Dishes

- 118 Neobiani Grilled Marinated Beef Slices
- 120 Galbi-gui Grilled Beef Short Ribs
- 122 Dwaeji-bossam Boiled Pork Wrapped with Napa Cabbage
- 124 Dak-jjim Braised Chicken in Soy Sauce
- 126 Dak-bokkeum-tang Spicy Braised Chicken
- 128 Godeungeo-gui Grilled Mackerel
- 130 Ojingeo-bokkeum Spicy Stir-fried Squid
- 132 Nokdu-bindae-tteok Mung Bean Pancake
- 134 Kimchi-jeon Kimchi Pancake
- 136 Saeu-jeon · Beoseot-jeon Pan-fried Shirmps · Pan-fried Mushrooms
- 138 Gujeol-pan Platter of Nine Delicacies
- 142 Tangpyeong-chae Mung Bean Jelly Mixed with Vegetables
- 144 Gungjung-tteok-bokki Royal Stir-fried Rice Cakes

Side Dishes

- 148 Saengseon-jorim Spicy Braised Fish
- 150 Saengseon-ganjang-jorim Glazed Fish in Soy Sauce
- 152 Dubu-jorim Braised Dubu in Soy Sauce
- 154 Dubu-kimchi Dubu with Stir-fried Kimchi
- 156 Gamja-jorim Braised Potatoes in Soy Sauce
- 158 Myeolchi-bokkeum Stir-fried Dried Anchovy
- 160 Sangchu-oi-saengchae Lettuce Salad with Cucumber
- 162 Baechu-geot-jeori Fresh Kimchi
- 164 Samsaek-namul Three-colored Seasoned Vegetables
- 166 Gosari-namul · Doraji-namul Seasoned Bracken · Seasoned Bellflower Roots
- 168 Gyeran-jjim Steamed Eggs
- 170 Gyeran-mari Rolled Omelet

Kimchi

- 174 Baechu-kimchi Whole Cabbage Kimchi
- 178 Baek-kimchi White Kimchi
- 180 Mat-kimchi (Seokbakji) Napa Cabbage and Radish Kimchi
- 182 Oi-so-bagi Cucumber Kimchi
- 184 Nabak-kimchi Water Kimchi
- 186 Dongchimi Radish Water Kimchi

Desserts

- 190 Songpyeon Half-moon Rice Cakes
- 192 Hwajeon Flower Rice Cakes
- 194 Maejakgwa Twisted Honey Cookies
- 196 Sujeonggwa Ginger and Cinnamon Punch
- 198 Omija-hwachae Omija Punch
- 200 Yuja-hwachae Yuja Punch

- 205 The Traditional Korean Table Setting
- 211 Korean Menu Suggestion
- 216 How to Enjoy Korean Food

- 218 References
- 220 Index

Nature's Influnce on Korean Cuisine

Understanding the environmental characteristics of Korea is necessary to see its influence on Korean cuisine and culture. Korea is located between the Chinese Mainland and the islands of Japan, and it therefore shares many cultural characteristics with the two countries. However, its unique climate and geography have also produced many differences.

1 Geography

Korea is located on the Korean Peninsula, which extends southward from the northeastern region of the Asian continental landmass. It shares its border with China and Russia to the north but is otherwise surrounded by water, resulting in a flourishing fishing industry. Forested, mountainous terrain covers 70 percent of the nation, yielding a variety of wild edible greens that are also grown in dry-field farms. Korea's major rivers, including the Nakdong River, the Han River and the Geum River, tend to flow westward along the mountain ranges, creating well-developed plains in the peninsula's western region. The conditions in the western and southern regions of the peninsula are therefore favorable to rice farms, while dry-field farms predominate in the northern and eastern regions. Korea's eastern coast has a smooth coastline, but the southern and western coasts have jagged coastlines with many islands. This provides an ideal environment for exploiting a rich variety of marine products.

Due to the varying geographical features and climates of the four regions of Korea, they have resulted in differing regional cuisines. Despite the development of transportation increasing contact between regions, and making local cultures less distinct, many of the unique local specialties and distinct styles of each province still remain.

2 Climate

The climate of Korea is characterized by four distinct seasons–spring, summer, autumn and winter–yielding a diverse array of seasonal foods. Even the same ingredients may have different tastes and nutrients in each season, which produces a variety of flavor variation within recipes. Unlike the abundant food materials available in the hot, humid summers and clear, dry springs and autumns, cold winters see Koreans eating dried vegetables and *kimchi* instead of fresh vegetables. *Jeotgal*, a salted fermented fish, was developed by the ancestors in the southern region of Korea as a way to preserve fish for a long period of time during the cold winters and hot summers. However, recent climate changes have introduced a subtropical climate to the peninsula, changing the types of seasonal food materials available.

Characteristics of Korean Cuisine

As previously mentioned Korea's environmental characteristics lend themselves to the diverse nature of the cuisine within the peninsula. Agricultural, livestock and marine products are all available in Korea. Koreans tend to eat cooked grains as a staple food and a number of side dishes made with vegetables, meats, and seafoods. The characteristics of Korean cuisine are described below.

1 Korean cuisine is based on two Oriental philosophies: 'medicine and food are one' and 'the eastern Yin and Yang philosophy and the Five Phases'

Korean cuisine is designed to achieve nutritional balance and a harmony between taste, texture, color, and other qualities because Korean believe that the foods work as a medicine in a body and concern the harmony of yin and yang. Typically, five to six seasonings are used to flavor a single dish to achieve a balanced taste, while five colors– red, green, yellow, white and black–are used to decorate the food.

2 Koreans enjoy a variety of ritual and seasonal foods

Korean enjoy seasonal foods with unique seasonal ingredients and also perform ancestral rituals with the foods. Foods are prepared according to each of the four seasons and 24 seasonal divisions, and are typically shared with family and neighbors.

3 Korean cuisine has a variety of grain dishes

Korea was traditionally an agricultural society that relied on cooked grains such as rice and barley as dietary staples. Other developed main dishes include porridge and noodles made from wheat or buckwheat, among other grains. The fermented foods are widely developed, such as grain-fermented foods; *ganjang* (soy sauce) and *gochu-jang* (red chili pepper paste) made from beans as well as traditional wines and beverages made from wheat, malt, cooked rice, cooked glutinous rice.

4 Korean dishes are distinctly categorized into main dishes and side dishes

The ordinary Korean meals are characterized by a number of *banchan* (side dishes) accompanying cooked rice. Side dishes are typically made from vegetables, meats and fishes cooked according to a variety of recipes. Side dishes can also include a bowl of soup or stew accompanied by one or two types of *kimchi* as the basic side dishes and additional 3 to 9 side dishes.

5 Korean dishes are rich in flavor because they use various seasonings and spices

A variety of seasonings, including *ganjang* (soy sauce), *seoltang* (sugar), *pa* (green onion), *maneul* (garlic), *kkae-sogeum* (toasted and crushed sesame seeds), *chamgireum* (sesame oil), *huchu* (ground black pepper) and *gochut-garu* (red chili pepper powder) can be used in a single Korean dish. These seasonings compliment the natural taste of the other ingredients and enrich their flavors.

6 Korean dishes require much time and effort

Unikely Western or Chinese foods, many Korean foods require the ingredients to be cut in specific ways to be easily eaten and to release their flavors differently. *Kimchi*, a well-known Korean food, and seasonings such as *ganjang* (soy sauce), *doenjang* (soybean paste) and *gochu-jang* (red chili pepper paste) require long periods of fermentation to produce their unique tastes and rich flavors. *Kimchi* is also internationally recognized for its nutritional benefits and considered as a super food.

Ingredients and Basic Techniques of Korean Cuisine

CHAPTER 1
Basic Ingredients of Korean Cuisine

The main ingredients in Korean food include grains, vegetables, fruits, meats, seafoods, seaweeds, and condiments. The descriptions below introduce their unique uses in Korean cooking.

1 Grains

The Koreans rice category includes glutinous and non-glutinous rices; the barley category consists of wheat, rye and oats; and the mixed crop category is composed of millet, barnyard millet, sorghum, corn and buckwheat. The following descriptions introduce the ingredients in *ogok-bap* (cooked five-grain rice) 78p and discuss white rice and brown rice.

Ssal (Short-grain rice and Glutinous rice) White rice falls into both *mepssal* (non-glutinous rice) and *chapssal* (glutinous rice). Non-glutinous rice contains two sub-groups; short-grain and long-grain. Most of Korean rice belongs to the short-grain rice sub-group.

Hyeonmi (Brown rice and Brown glutinous rice) This rice varies depending on the degree of milling and is categorized as white, 9 milling, 7 milling or brown rice. The more the rice is milled, the whiter and softer it becomes. However, whiter rice is less nutritious because the milling process removes minerals and vitamins contained inside the hull and the eye.

Jo (Millet) There are glutinous and non-glutinous varieties of millet, although typically, only the former is used in food. Glutinous millet is the raw material for rice and porridge dishes, taffy and liquor.

Susu (Sorghum) Glutinous sorghum is rich in protein and fat. Traditionally, sorghum is used in red bean rice cakes, which are commonly made for a child's 1-year birthday or 100th-day celebration.

Bori (Barley) Barley includes whole barley and naked barley. Barley grain is rich in cellulose even after milling and is difficult to digest. Barley is processed and sold as pressed or broken barley. It provides supplementary nutrients, such as vitamins and minerals if mixed and cooked with rice.

Pat (Red beans) Red bean rice cakes are served at shamanistic rituals because the red color is thought to expel ghosts. It is also a tradition to cook *patjuk* (red bean porridge) 84p on *Dongji* (winter solstice). Red beans are also used to make rice cake fillings.

Kong (Beans) Beans are categorized by color as white, yellow, brown or black and are processed to create foods such as *dubu* (tofu), soy milk, soy sauce, bean sprouts, bean powders, soybeans and rich soybean paste. Beans are one of the safest Korean foods and are the best protein supplier among plant-based proteins.

Nokdu (Mung beans) Mung beans are primarily used to create starch powders. They contain protein and have a mild sweet flavor. Their sprouts are used to make *namul* (seasoned mung bean sprouts) as a side dish. These beans are also soaked and ground to make *nokdu-bindae-tteok* (mung bean pancake) 132p, mixed with rice to make mung bean porridge or mixed with cooked rice to make rice cake filling, tea or liquor.

2 Vegetables and Fruits

Korean side dishes are primarily made from vegetables and fruits that are rich in vitamins, minerals, and cellulose. Koreans began to consume more meat following the introduction of Western dietary culture. However, Korean meals still include many vegetables, such as *kimchi*, seasoned vegetables, and salads. There is unique dietary culture that wraps the meat with leafy vegetables, as well. Korean food is considered as a healthy cuisine because diverse range of vegetables are used and can be cooked in many different ways.

Baechu (Napa cabbage) Napa cabbage, the main ingredient of *baechu-kimchi* (the most iconic *kimchi*), is widely used for *guk* (soups), *geot-jeori* (fresh kimchi) 162p and *ssam* (wraps) and contains more protein, vitamin C and minerals than other vegetables. The best cabbages are those that feel heavy and have a high density, a sweet taste and thin leaves.

Sangchu (Lettuce) Lettuce is typically eaten raw, but it is also used to make *geot-jeori* (fresh kimchi), which has a soft and crispy texture. Koreans traditionally wrap rice and meat in wide, green lettuce to create a balanced meal rich in vitamins, minerals and cellulose, which are difficult to obtain from only grains or meat.

Sigeumchi (Spinach) Spinach is used as a seasoned vegetable 164p and as an ingredient in *doenjang-guk* (soybean soup) 102p or *gimbap* (toasted laver rolls) 70p. The best spinach has a short stem with a sweet flavor and odor. Spinach is used to make seasoned side dishes.

Kkannip (Perilla leaf) Perilla leaf is an indispensable vegetable ingredient in various dishes because of its fresh aroma and flavor. Fresh perilla leaf is used in *ssam* (wraps) or is salted or steamed as a side dish. The best perilla leaves are soft and dark green in color with a wet stem. Perilla leaves contain many minerals, including potassium and calcium.

Ssukgat (Crown daisy) The crown daisy has a pleasant odor and is used with lettuce in *ssam* wraps or in seasoned vegetables. The crown daisy must be boiled slightly to preserve its fresh odor before being served in spicy stews, in broth or in hot pots.

Minari (Korean watercress) Korean watercress has a fresh flavor and is typically parboiled with fresh or seasoned vegetables. The leaf and the stem are edible, but Koreans conventionally use the latter. Its stem is fried and used in *gomyeong* (garnishes) 26p or *jeon* (pan-fried dishes). It is also slightly boiled in fish broths, stews or spicy stews to remove any fishy odors.

Buchu (Chives) Chives are used as a *kimchi* ingredient in *buchu-kimchi*, *oi-so-bagi* (cucumber kimchi) 182p or as an ingredient in broths or stews. It has a strong scent that is similar to garlic, green onion or ginger and is frequently used as a seasoning because of its ability to remove fatty or fishy odor.

Hobak (Korean squash) The Korean squash types are categorized according to species and maturity and include *ae-hobak* (Korean young squash) and *neulgeun-hobak* (aged squash). Side dishes are primarily made using firm and shiny young squash. Squashes are widely used in *jjigae* (stews), such as *doenjang-jjigae* (soybean paste stew) 106p, in *bokkeum* (stir-fried dishes) and in *jeon* (pan-fried dishes). Aged squash and/or sweet pumpkins are steamed or used to make *juk* (porridge) 82p and *jeon* (pan-fried dishes).

Gochu (Chili pepper) Chili pepper is the most widely used vegetable in side dishes and seasonings. Fresh red chili peppers may be green or red. The former has a spicy, sweet taste and is served with *ssam-jang* (seasoned soybean paste), and used in stew or salad. It is also used to make *gochu-jeon* (pan-fried chili pepper) by removing the pepper's core and filling it with a meat filling. Red chili peppers are used as an ingredient in stews and used as a red garnish. *Geon-gochu* refers to dried whole red chili pepper, and *sil-gochu* refers to thin dried red chili pepper threads. *Sil-gochu* is generally used as a red garnish. The dried red chili pepper is ground to make *gochut-garu* (red chili pepper powder). It is more difficult to choose the correct type of red chili pepper in other countries, where many varieties are available.

Oi (Cucumbers) Cucumbers are used in side dishes such as *oiji* (pickled cucumber), *oi-naengguk* (chilled cucumber soup) 104p, *oi-namul* (seasoned cucumber) or as garnishes for noodles such as *mul-naengmyeon* (buckwheat noodles in chilled broth) 86p and *bibim-naengmyeon* (spicy buckwheat noodles) 88p. Because cucumbers are moist, they are also used in summer salads to provide supplementary water, *oi-so-bagi* (cucumber kimchi) 182p is a representative summer *kimchi*.

Mu (White radish) White radishes are an important ingredient in *baechu-kimchi* (fermented whole cabbage) 174p. Some types of *kimchi* are made using only white radishes, such as *kkakdugi* (diced radish *kimchi*) and *dongchimi* (radish water kimchi) 186p. White radishes are used in various dishes, such as soups, seasoned vegetables, braised dishes, and picked vegetables. Korean white radishes are extremely juicy and have a sweet flavor; they are often eaten fresh.

Danggeun (Carrots) Carrots are considerably used in Korean cuisines, such as *bibimbap* (rice mixed with vegetables and beef) 52p, *japchae* (stir-fried sweet potato noodles with vegetables) 68p, and *dak-jjim* (braised chicken in soy sauce) 124p. As carrots contain a large amount of beta-carotene, the absorption of beta-carotene into the body is enhanced when the carrots are cooked in oil.

Doraji (Bellflower roots) The best bellflower roots have a white, straight, elastic root. Fresh bellflower roots are sliced and used in *saengchae* or *sukchae namul* (fresh or cooked salads) and as a seasoned vegetable or is preserved in honey. Dried bellflower roots are used in *guk* (soups) and *japchae* (stir-fried sweet potato noodles and vegetables) 68p.

Gosari (Bracken) Bracken is an alpine plant that grows in wet environments. Dried bracken is boiled and then used in *namul* (seasoned vegetables) and *guk* (soups).

Kong-namul · Sukju (Bean sprouts · Mung bean sprouts) Bean sprouts are cultivated by planting the beans in homes and are frequently served during all seasons. Bean sprouts contain vitamin C and are a good vitamin source during the winter. When cooked in broth, bean sprouts are also used to ease hangovers and fatigue because they are rich in aspartic acid. Mung bean sprouts are cultivated by planting the green beans. However, Koreans eat mung bean sprouts as a seasoned vegetable after parboiling them or use them in *bindae-tteok* (mung bean pancake) 132p or *tangpyeong-chae* (mung bean jelly mixed with vegetables) 142p.

Beoseot (Mushrooms) Koreans primarily use *pyogo* (shiitake) mushrooms. They are used in *jeongol* (hot pots), *guk* (soups) and *jeon* (pan-fried dishes). Dried mushrooms have a rich odor and taste, and the water used to soak *pyogo* mushrooms is used to make *guk* (soups) and *jjigae* (stews).

The pine mushroom is best during autumn because of its rich flavor. Although expensive, it is suitable for roasting and for hot pots and rice dishes. The tree ear is a dark brown mushroom that grows on trees in the shape of an eardrum. It is used in soups, noodles and vegetable dishes and is often steamed. Manna lichen is black and is primarily used as a garnish. Many more mushrooms, including oyster mushrooms, king oyster mushrooms and winter mushrooms, are currently used widely in Korean foods such as *jjigae* (stews), *namul* (seasoned vegetables), *jeon* (pan-fried dishes) and *japchae* (stir-fried sweet potato noodles and vegetables) 68p.

Gyeongwa-ryu (Nuts) The nuts used in Korean food include *bam* (chestnuts), *eunhaeng* (gingko nuts), *hodu* (walnuts) and *jat* (pine nuts). These nuts are especially used as garnishes. Chestnuts are used as an ingredient of *galbi-jjim* (braised short ribs in soy sauce) 60p and *samgye-tang* (ginseng chicken soup) 114p. When gingko nuts are used for food, only the core is used after peeling off the external and internal skin, reducing their toxicity. Roasting or heating ginko nuts releases a distinct flavor. They are often eaten pan-fried or roasted rather than fresh. Walnuts are eaten fresh and added to various foods or snacks. Pine nuts are used as a tea or *hwachae* (punch) garnish, added to *tteok* (rice cakes), eaten as snacks or made into porridge. Pine nut porridge is consumed to promote stamina.

Bae (Pears) Pears are the most widely used fruit in Korean cuisine. They are juicier and sweeter than Western pears and are recognized worldwide for their crispy texture. Pears are either eaten as a dessert or used as a garnish on *naengmyeon* (cold buckwheat noodle dishes) 86p. In addition, ground pear is used in *bulgogi* (grilled marinated beef) 58p and steamed pork rib seasonings to soften the meat. Pear is also served as a garnish in *omija-hwachae* (omija punch) 198p or *yuja-hwachae* (yuja punch) 200p.

Yuja *Yuja* is a type of citrus. Being aromatic and rich in vitamin C, it is ideal for preventing illness. The *yuja*'s skin, which accounts for half of its weight, is used for cooking, but the flesh is too sour to eat. The skin is often marinated in sugar and used to make tea, *hwachae* (punch) or *tteok* (rice cakes).

Omija *Omija* simultaneously tastes sweet, sour, bitter, salty and spicy. Dried *omija* containing abundant flesh and a red color are preferred. Punch is made using *omija* soaked in cold water and mixed with honey or sugar. It is also boiled with nuts, jujube and a dash of ginseng to make tea or liquor.

Seokryu (Pomegranate) Pomegranate contains estrogenic hormones and, therefore, is especially beneficial for women. The mature fruit tastes sour and sweet and is sometimes mixed with grains to decorate *hwachae* (punch) because of its beautiful red color.

Daechu (Jujubes) Jujubes are indispensable for rites of passage because of these symbolic association with fertility. It is used in Oriental medicine in tea, along with ginseng and other medicinal herbs, to promote stamina. Sliced jujube is served in *sujeonggwa* (ginger and cinnamon punch) 196p or tea, used as a rice cake ingredient, eaten as a snack or used in ginseng chicken soup. Jujubes are similar in appearance to dates but are not as sweet. Dried jujubes are also used for cooking.

Gotgam (Dried persimmon) Dried persimmon is a preferred snack because of its sweet taste and is also used to make *sujeonggwa* (ginger and cinnamon punch) 196p or *gotgam-ssam* (walnuts wrapped in persimmons). To dry persimmons, Koreans peel off the skin before the persimmon is ripe. Then they skew the flesh, dry it in the sun, trim it and dry it again until white glucose powder appears on the surface.

3 Meat

Meat, including beef, pork and chicken, was once rare in the ancient agricultural society of Korea. Meat was primarily consumed only in the royal court or among nobles. It was eaten grilled, steamed or in steamed slices. It is important to understand which cooking methods are appropriate for each cut of meat.

So-gogi (Beef) Beef is the most widely used meat in Korean dishes. It contains various nutrients, including protein, vitamin B complex and iron, and has a delicious flavor. Its quality and taste largely depend on the species, sex and age of the animal. The best beef displays evenly distributed marbling on the surface that resembles frost. Beef quality and freshness are important, but it is most important to use an appropriate cooking method for each cut of beef.

Dwaeji-gogi (Pork) Pork lends itself to a variety of cooking methods, including *gui* (grilling), *jjim* (steaming), *pyeonyuk* (slicing), *jorim* (braising) and *bokkeum* (stir-frying). Because pork meat is tender and palatable, it is well-suited for spicy seasoned dishes, such as *jeyuk-bokkeum* (spicy stir-fried pork) 62p and *dwaeji-galbi-jjim* (braised pork rib). *Samgyeopsal-gui* (grilled pork belly), in particular, is extremely popular in Korea.

Dak-gogi (Chicken) Chicken is a good source of protein that contains less fat than other meats and is easily digested. *Samgye-tang* (ginseng chicken soup) 114p is a representative stamina-providing food used to manage the summer heat. It is popular as a delivery or street food in dishes such as fried chicken, *maekom-dak-gangjeong* (deep-fried chicken with sweet and spicy sauce) 74p, and *dak-jjim* (braised chicken in soy sauce) 124p. Additionally, it is served as *kal-guksu* (noodles in broth) 94p or porridge made using chicken broth.

4 Seafood

Seafood is an essential protein source in Korea, which is surrounded on 3 sides by the sea. Via maritime activities, Koreans harvest cold and warm fish and mackerel, pollock and squid. However, the availability of many species is in flux due to changing water temperatures caused by climate change. Koreans traditionally enjoyed seafood in side dishes. Rather than consumed raw, it was typically grilled, steamed or boiled in soybean sauce. Traditional Korean seafood dishes include the flesh, eggs and intestines of seafood.

Myeongtae (Pollock) Pollock is also called fresh pollock, frozen pollock, dried pollock, pollock dried by the wind or kodari, depending on the province. Frozen pollock, which has a longer shelf life than fresh pollock, is inexpensive and is primarily used in side dishes, such as spicy stews or jorim.

Daegu (Codfish) Codfish resembles pollock but has a much larger mouth and a longer body. It is pale gray, lives in cold water and has white flesh and a mild taste. It is stewed, cooked in hot pots, braised, or pan-fried in assorted dishes and soups.

Galchi (Hairtail) Hairtail resembles a long sword and has a white color and no scales. It is typically grilled or cooked as *saengseon-jorim* (spicy braised fish) 148p. It contains an average amount of fat and has a good flavor.

Gajami (Halibut) Halibut is a flat fish with eyes only on the right side of its body. Fresh halibut is served raw and cooked via *gui* (grilling), *jorim* (braising), *and jjim* (steamed). Alternatively, dried halibut is grilled with salt seasoning.

Megi (Catfish) Catfish is popular for braised dishes and spicy stews. It is high in protein and vitamins and is known as a nutritious fish. It is used in various dishes, including *guk* (soups), *twigim* (deep-fried) and *gui* (grilled). As a white-meat fish, catfish is more common in other countries than in Korea.

Godeungeo (Mackerel) Mackerel is a representative blue colored fish in Korea. Fresh-caught mackerel is consumed raw but more often served as *godeungeo-gui* (grilled mackerel) 128p or braised for *jorim* dishes.

Samchi (Spanish mackerel) Exhibiting a long, spindle-like shape and a silver-gray color, spotted mackerel has white flesh and a mild flavor. It is eaten raw, grilled and used in *saengseon-ganjang-jorim* (glazed fish in soy sauce) 150p.

Yeonche-ryu (Cephalopods) Cephalopods are high in protein and low in calories. *Ojingeo* (squid) is parboiled and served with *cho-gochu-jang* (red chili pepper paste with vinegar) 46p or used in *bokkeum* (stir-fried dishes), *jorim* (braised dishes), *jjigae* (stews) and *twigim* (fried dishes). Stir-fried *nakji* (small octopus) is a popular dish among Koreans. Before cooking *muneo* (octopus), the ink sac is removed. Then, the remaining octopus is rubbed with salt and parboiled. Octopus is served as *suk-hoe* (parboiled octopus), *cho-muchim* (salad with vinegar dressing), *jorim* (braised dishes) and *bokkeum* (stir-fried dishes). Dried octopus is considered as a delicacy.

Gapgak-ryu (Crustaceans) *Saeu* (shrimp) and *ge* (crab) are popular crustaceans used in Korean cuisines. There are many types of shrimps, and they are categorized into 3 groups according to size: large, medium, and small. Large shrimp is prepared by *jjim* (steaming), *gui* (grilling), *twigim* (deep-frying) or *saeu-jeon* (pan-frying) 136p. Medium shrimp is boiled and served with salad. Small shrimp is dried or used to make salted shrimp. Koreans eat both sea crabs and river crabs. Crab is steamed, used in *guk* (soups) or *jjigae* (stews), or used to make soy sauce-marinated crab dishes. The Korean crab has a firm shell and sweet flesh.

Jogae (Clam) Clams develop a delicious flavor after being boiled and are used in *jeongol* (hot pots), *guk* (soups) and *jjigae* (stews). The corb-shell clam has a fresh taste and is ideal for clear broths. The small Manila clam is used to make broth for *kal-guksu* (noodles in broth) 94p, and the flesh is used for *jorim* (braising) and *jeon* (pan-frying).

Myeolchi (Anchovy) Most anchovies are steamed and dried or are used in salted anchovy dishes. Dried anchovies are categorized according to size. Large anchovies are used to make broth, and small- and medium-sized anchovies are used in *myeolchi-bokkeum* (stir-fried dried anchovy) 158p. Anchovies were Koreans' primary source of calcium when milk was rare, and they have recently become popular as a side dish to serve to children. Salted anchovies are used to season *kimchi* or other dishes.

5 Seaweed

Seaweed is touted as a low-calorie, healthy food that is rich in minerals. Laver, seaweed and kelp are popular in Korean cuisine. Fresh seaweed and kelp are used for *ssam* (wraps), but seaweed is most often eaten dried.

Gim (Laver) Laver is prepared by toasting dried laver with sesame or perilla oil and salt. It is a generally popular side dish and is easily found in the supermarket or market. Toasted laver is used to garnish *tteokguk* (sliced rice cake soup) 96p and *gimbap* (toasted laver rolls) 70p. Laver chips are applied to rice cakes using glutinous paste and are dried and then fried in oil.

Miyeok (Seaweed) Dried seaweed is soaked in water and used for dishes such as *miyeok-guk* (seaweed soup) 100p, seasoned vegetables, *ssam* (wraps) and chilled soup. Traditionally, Koreans eat seaweed soup for breakfast on their birthday; this soup can be made using a variety of ingredients, including beef, oysters and shellfish. Seaweed is high in iodine and calcium and is especially beneficial for pregnant women because it stabilizes metabolism. It is traditional for a Korean mother to eat seaweed soup for one month or more after delivering a baby to recover her health.

Dasima (Kelp) Kelp is high in potassium, calcium, iodine and vitamin A and is used to make savory broth. Dried kelp is thick and glossy; the best kelp is covered with white powder. Kelp is used with dried anchovies to make broth. This broth tastes especially fresh when used for white radish soup.

6 Yangnyeom and Gomyeong (Seasonings and Garnishes)

Yangnyeom (Seasonings)

Seasonings draw out the unique flavors of a dish's ingredients, and various seasonings are used to create unique flavor combinations. Seasonings primarily consist of condiments and spices. Condiments are ingredients that contain salty, sweet, sour, spicy and bitter flavors. Spices lend their own scent to a dish, and spicy, bitter and crispy pastes can remove certain odors or enhance an ingredient's original flavor.

Sogeum (Salt) Salt is a fundamental condiment for flavoring food. The salts that are most commonly used in Korean cuisine are *cheonilyeom* (natural sea salt) and *kkot-sogeum* (coarse salt/refined salt). The former is typically produced in salt fields in the West and South Seas, which are shallow and have large tidal differences and is used to pickle fish and make *kimchi*. Table salt does not come from salt fields but rather is produced via ion exchange. It is highly refined and is soft. It is also used to season foods and is typically placed on the table.

Gangjang (Soy sauce) Soy sauce, an essential flavoring ingredient used in traditional Korean fermented food, is made from soybean paste and fermented beans. China and Japan also use soy sauce, but the sauces used in these countries contain different flavors and ingredients. *Guk-ganjang* (soy sauce for soup) and *jin-ganjang* (soy sauce) are typically used in Korean cuisine. In this book, *jin-ganjang* is presented simply as "soy sauce". *Guk-ganjang*, which is saltier than *ganjang*, is essentially used in *guk* (soups), *jjigae* (stews) and *namul* (seasoned vegetable dishes). *Ganjang* is also used in *jorim* (braised dish) and meat dishes. This sauce is used to season foods, and is mixed with vinegar to make *cho-ganjang*.

Doenjang (Soybean paste) To make *doenjang*, a fermented soybean lump is made from white beans and is soaked in saltwater for 40 days. Soy sauce is made from the broth that forms from the salt water-soaked bean elements, whereas the solid lump is made into *doenjang*. This paste is used as a condiment and is a good source of protein. *Doenjang* is primarily used to flavor *doenjang-guk* (soybean paste soup) or *doenjang-jjigae* (soybean paste stew) 106p. It is also a primary ingredient in *ssam-jang* (seasoned soybean paste) 48p, which is served with lettuce or pumpkin wraps. Recently, several varieties of mixed pastes have become available on the market because few families make *ganjang* or *doenjang* at home.

Gochu-jang (Red chili pepper paste) This unique condiment of Korea is made with fermented rice, flour, red chili pepper powder, taffy oil, soy lump powder and salt. Its sweetness comes from fermented rice; its freshness is derived from beans; its spiciness originates from red chili pepper and its saltiness comes from salt. It is used as a seasoning in various Korean dishes, including seasoned vegetables, braised and grilled meat; it is also used to improve the flavor of stews. *Gochu-jang* is used as a sauce in *bibimbap* 152p, *bibim-naengmyeon* (spicy buckwheat noodles) 88p and *cho-gochu-jang* (red chili pepper paste with vinegar) 46p and is served with raw fish. Spicy sauces made using red chili pepper paste are the secret ingredients in street foods such as *maekom-dak-gangjeong* (deep-fried chicken with sweet and spicy sauce) 74p and *tteok-bokki* (stir-fried rice cakes with gochu-jang sauce) 72p.

Gochut-garu (Red chili pepper powder) Red chili pepper powder is the most widely used spicy flavoring in Korean cuisines, and the texture of the powder used depends on the dish. Coarse *gochut-garu* is used in *kimchi*, and fine *gochut-garu* is used as a general seasoning.

Chamgireum · Deulgireum (Sesame oil · Perilla oil) Sesame oil is produced by roasting sesame seeds and is widely used in combination with many ingredients and cooking methods. In particular, sesame oil improves the flavor of seasoned vegetables, *bibimbap* 52p and meat seasonings. This oil is also used to imbue fresh food with its strong flavor and scent. Perilla oil is made by roasting and squeezing perilla seeds and is primarily used to stir-fry vegetables and seaweed. Both oils contain many unsaturated fatty acids and have low boiling points, making them unsuitable for frying or making pan-frying dishes.

Sikcho (Vinegar) Vinegar adds a sour taste to salads and *oi-naengguk* (chilled cucumber soup) 104p. The vinegar used in Korean food is brewed by fermenting grains or fruits. Brown rice and apple vinegars are the most common vinegar.

Kkul (Honey) This natural sweetener is made by bees and is the oldest known food, dating from the Paleolithic era. It ranges from transparent to opaque and may contain a white sediment. Its flavor and scent are sweet, but it is primarily used in snacks, rice cakes or preserved snacks rather than in expensive foods. Taffy and grain syrup were once used to sweeten dishes, but now corn syrup predominates.

Jocheong (Grain syrup) This thick, watery taffy is made by saccharifying grains into taffy oil and subjecting the resulting product to prolonged boiling. The yellow color and unique scent of the taffy remain. Currently, grain syrup is primarily used in traditional Korean snacks and side dishes.

Pa (Green onion) Along with garlic and green onions are the representative seasoning vegetable in Korea and are used in most Korean foods. There are several types of green onions, and they are generally categorized as thick or thin. *Daepa* (thick or large green onion) is sliced or minced into various foods; only the white part is used when mincing. *Silpa* (green onion or scallion) is used in various foods, such as *pa-kimchi*, *jeon* (pan-fried dishes) and garnishes.

Maneul (Garlic) Minced garlic is an important seasoning in most Korean foods. For convenience, minced garlic can be prepared in advance and then stored in the refrigerator and used as needed. Whole or ground garlic is used when steaming meat or fish, and it removes the odor of the meat or fish due to its unique taste and scent. Whole garlic is also boiled with chicken to create a sweet flavor.

Saenggang (Ginger) Ginger is a root vegetable used as a seasoning. Its flavor is both bitter and spicy, and its strong scent removes the odor from *saengseon-jorim* (spicy braised fish) 148p or braised pork. It facilitates digestion and improves blood circulation. Ginger is boiled to make ginger tea or liquor.

Huchu (Pepper) Pepper removes the odor from fish or meat, improves a dish's flavor and scent and stimulates the appetite. Because of its strong scent, black pepper is suitable for meat and dark-colored foods; white pepper, due to its mild taste and scent, is suitable for white-fleshed fish and vegetables.

Gyeoja (Mustard) Mustard powder is mixed with warm water to add a spicy flavor and is then mixed with vinegar, sugar and salt to make mustard sauce. It is also mixed with mustard salad and *naengmyeon* (cold buckwheat noodles) 86p.

Saeu-jeot (Salted shrimp) This seasoning is made with small salted shrimp and is primarily used to make *kimchi*. It is also used as a salt substitute to soups, stews and vegetables and has a more complex flavor than salt. It is particularly well-suited for Korean young squash, *dubu* (tofu) and pork and is often used to make *dubu jjigae* (tofu stew) or stir-fried Korean young squash.

Myeolchi-aekjeot (Anchovy sauce) Made from the clear sauce collected from the anchovy-fermenting process, fermented anchovy sauce is used for *kimchi*, salads, soups or stews as a substitute for soybean sauce. New varieties of fermented sauces are currently being sold, including anchovy, sand eel and tuna.

Kkae (Sesame) Sesame oil is made by rinsing sesame seeds in water, frying them in a thick pot while stirring with a wooden spatula, adding a dash of salt before cooling, and grinding them in a large mortar. Whole sesame seeds can also be used as a seasoning after being stir-fried. Fine sesame seeds can be made by peeling off the inner shell.

Gomyeong (Garnish)

Garnishes are used to decorate food and give it a pleasing appearance and color. In Korea, garnishes are sometimes referred to as *utgi* or *kkumi*. A basic garnish consists of 5 colors: red, green, yellow, white and black. This combination is based on the philosophy of Yin-Yang and the Five Phases and relies on the garnishes' natural colors.

Red garnish Red garnishes are made with red chili peppers, threaded red chili peppers, jujubes and carrots. Fresh peppers may be used, but dried red chili peppers can also be used after being ground and slightly parboiled. Fine peppers are sliced into 2-4-cm strips and used in seasoned vegetables. The red dried jujube, after being sliced and deseeded, is used in *bossam kimchi* (wrapped *kimchi*) and *baek-kimchi* (white kimchi) 178p and is sliced in the shape of a flower to garnish *sujeonggwa* (ginger and cinnamon punch) 196p and tea. Carrots must be sliced and slightly stir-fried before use.

Green garnish Green garnishes are created using thick green onion, green onion, gingko nuts, Korean watercress, crown daisy, Korean young squash, cucumber and green chili pepper. Both types of green onion are used to garnish various foods, such as noodle dishes, soups, stews, hot pots and braised dishes. As a garnish, green onion removes the odor from ingredients. Cucumbers and Korean young squash are slightly stir-fried before being used as garnishes, but Korean watercress and crown daisy are served fresh with stews and hot pots. Korean watercress skewers are made by skewering the watercress stem, coating it with beaten egg yolks and shaping it into diamonds or rectangular shapes, for use as a garnish for stews, hot pots and *sinseollo* (royal hot pot). Gingko nuts are used as a garnish for hot pots, braised dishes and *sinseollo* after being peeled, stir-fried in oil in a hot pan and rubbed with dry cloth or kitchen towel to peel off the inner skin.

Yellow garnish Yellow garnishes for various foods are made using egg yolks by separating the egg whites, beating and pan-frying in a lightly greased skillet, followed by cutting into diamonds or rectangular shapes or slicing thinly.

White garnish White garnishes can be used with thinly pan-fried egg whites, sesame, nuts and pine nuts. Thinly pan-fried egg whites are prepared similarly to a yellow garnish and then cut into diamonds or rectangular shapes for *jjim* (braised dishes) or *jeongol* (hot pots) or thinly sliced for *namul* (seasoned vegetables) 164p or *gujeol-pan* (platter of nine delicacies) 138p. They may also be sliced and used to garnish seasoned vegetable dishes or *gujeol-pan* 138p. Sesame seeds 47p are used for various foods to enhance their odor and flavor. Toasted and peeled sesame seeds are prepared by peeling the sesame seeds and toasting the seeds in a skillet without oil. Unlike uncooked sesame seeds, toasted and peeled sesame seeds are white and savory and are used for *namul* (seasoned vegetables), *japchae* (stir-fried sweet potato noodles and vegetables) 68p, *jeok* (skewer dishes), and *gui* (grilled dishes). Whole pine nuts are added to drinks, such as *hwachae* (punch) or tea. They may also be sliced in half and used with rice cakes or snacks. Ground pine nuts are used as a garnish for side dishes. These nuts may be sliced or cut after being peeled and used as garnishes for *bossam kimchi* (wrapped kimchi), *baek-kimchi* (white *kimchi*), mustard salads and cold salads, as well as for *ttoek* (rice cakes) and traditional Korean desserts.

Black garnish Black garnishes are made from beef, *pyogo* (shiitake) mushrooms, black sesame and manna lichen. Beef flesh, after the fat is removed, is sliced or minced, seasoned and fried before being used to garnish *tteokguk* (sliced rice cake soup) 96p, *guksu* (noodles) or *bibimbap* 52p. Beef may also be sliced or stir-fried and served as a garnish for noodles or rice cake soup. Manna lichen is soaked in water, trimmed, rolled and sliced or fried with egg whites. It has a unique color and gives a dish a sense of luxury, but it is difficult to find. *Pyogo* mushrooms are dark brown and create rich flavors due to their unique scent and flavor. They are used as a black garnish when sliced, seasoned and added to *janchi-guksu* (noodles in anchovy broth) 90p or *bibimbap* 52p. Similar to whole sesame seeds, black sesame seeds can be fried and added to food. They can also be ground and used as garnish for *tteok* (rice cakes).

7 Miscellaneous

This section introduces noodles and rice cakes, which are served in place of cooked rice, *dubu* (tofu) or *muk* (jellied food) and are widely used as side dishes.

Guksu (Noodles)

The noodles used in Korean cuisine consist of plain noodles, soup noodles made of flour, cold noodles made from buckwheat flour and sweet potato noodles made from sweet potato starch. Noodles are generally categorized as dry or fresh.

Somyeon · Kal-guksu (Wheat flour noodles) These noodles are distinguished based on their thickness. The wheat flour noodle has a 1-mm diameter and is primarily used for *janchi-guksu* (noodles in anchovy broth) 90p and *goldong-myeon* (noodles mixed with vegetables and beef) 92p. Noodles displaying flat, wide surface are referred to as *kal-guksu* (noodles in broth) 94p. These noodles are boiled in anchovy or chicken broth or are used as a hot pot ingredient. Dried noodles are readily available in Asian grocery stores.

Naengmyeon (Buckwheat noodles or Cold noodles) Naengmyeon is made from buckwheat. They are typically prepared with chilled beef broth or mixed with *dongchimi* (radish water kimchi) 186p broth. Sliced meat, pears and boiled eggs are prepared as garnishes. The noodles may be dried or fresh, and the latter are sold with a broth mix that allows *naengmyeon* to be easily prepared at home.

Dangmyeon (Sweet potato noodles) Sweet potato noodles are generally made from sweet potato starch and are used in *japchae* (stir-fried sweet potato noodles and vegetables) 68p and in *mandu* (dumplings) 56p.

Tteok (Rice cakes)

It is a Korean tradition to make rice cakes and share them with neighbors on special occasions. Rice cakes are made for large events and rites of passage, such as 100th-day celebrations, first birthday parties, marriages, grand openings, acceptance to school or earning a job. Glutinous and short-grain rice are the main ingredients of rice cakes.

Mepssal-garu (Short-grain rice flour)
Short-grain rice cakes, which is unsweet *garae-tteock*, are normally served as a meal. The rice cakes used in *tteokguk* (sliced rice cake soup) 96p are made by slicing a roll of appropriately hardened rice cake. The cake used for *tteok-bokki* (stir-fried rice cake with gochu-jang sauce) 72p originates from a thin roll that is cut into bite-sized pieces. *Songpyeon* (half-moon rice cakes) 190p is another type of rice cake that is made from short-grain rice.

Chapssal-garu (Glutinous rice flour) Rice cakes such as *hwajeon* (flower rice cakes) 192p are made from glutinous rice flour. The cooked glutinous rice flour is sticky when pulled with the hands. Wet glutinous rice flour is made by soaking rice in water for over 5 hours and then draining the water and grinding the rice into flour. Dried glutinous flour, which is easily found in the grocery stores needs more water than wet glutinous rice flour when making rice cakes.

Dubu (Tofu)

Dubu is made by soaking beans in water, grinding and boiling them and then removing the *biji* (bean-curd dregs) and solidifying with the remaining using inorganic salt. *Dubu* is referred to "beef from the field" because it contains vegetable protein and is frequently used as a major protein source in China, Japan and Korea. It has a soft texture and is easy to digest, so it is good for children and the elderly as a meal. It has almost no odor and enhances the flavors of other ingredients. It is frequently fried or used in *jorim* (braised dishes), *guk* (soups) and *jjigae* (stews). There are many types of *dubu*, and they are categorized according to the processing method:

Pan-dubu (Firm and medium-soft tofu) *Pan-dubu*, which is typically sold in a rectangular pan, has a firm texture and is frequently used in various Korean foods. It is categorized into 2 groups, for *jeon* (pan-fried dishes), and for *guk* (soups) and *jjigae* (stews), depending on its use. Essentially, *dubu* for pan-fried dishes has a harder texture than *dubu* for soups or stews.

Yeon-dubu (Silk tofu) *Yeon-dubu* contains more moisture than firm *dubu* and has a soft and silky texture. It is served as a side dish seasoned with *ganjang* (soy sauce) or as a salad.

Sun-dubu (Soft tofu) *Sun-dubu* is made without removing the moisture from solidified soymilk and is used in *sundubu-jjigae* (spicy soft dubu stew) 54p.

Muk (Jellied food)

Muk is a traditional Korean food made by extracting starches from grains or fruits, bring to a boil with water, and then thickening. It is not especially flavorful, but its unique texture stimulates the appetite when served with vegetables or seasonings.

Cheongpo-muk (Mung bean jelly) This is made from mung bean starch, which is grown in the spring. It is white and clean and has a smooth, soft texture. When mixed with Korean watercress or mung bean sprouts, it becomes a good source of vitamins. It is often seasoned with *cho-ganjang* (red chili pepper paste with vinegar) or with salt and sesame oil to give it a mild flavor.

Dotori-muk (Acorn jelly) This jelly is made by collecting acorns in the mountains in the autumn, removing the shell, soaking them in water to remove their bitter taste, grinding them and cooking the residue. It has a unique taste and is served with seasoned *ganjang* (soy sauce) 45p and vegetables such as cucumbers or crown daisies.

CHAPTER 2

Shopping for Korean Ingredients in Other Countries

Korean cuisine has gained world-wide attention as healthful foods because of the increased number of grains and vegetables compared to Western foods, as well as the scientifically proven benefits of fermented foods. As purchasing ingredients is an important part of cooking Korean food, this chapter provides tips on shopping for ingredients easily in the Americas.

1 Korean Markets in the Americas

Korean grocery stores in the Amricas include Hannam Supermarket (www.hannamsm.com), H-Mart (www.hmart.com), Galleria Market (www.galleriamarket.com), Hanyang Mart (www.hanyangmart.com), and Koa Mart (www.kgrocer.com). These stores provide vegetables, meat, fish and shellfish at reasonable prices compared to the major supermarkets in the nation, and are gaining increasing popularity among locals. Most of the food ingredients used in Korean food are available in these store, and shoppers can conveniently taste the food products in demonstration and sample areas. The large variety of ramen, sweets, drinks, frozen foods and sauces are enough to make you feel like you are in a supermarket in Korea, and diverse cooking utensils are also available at the stores.

If there is no Korean food store near your location, you may visit Asian grocery stores to buy alternative products. However, as previously mentioned, because tastes of condiments or *dubu* (tofu) products may vary across the originating countries, you need to pay attention when choosing ingredients. Also local stores in the Americas, Trader Joe's (www.traderjoes.com) offers Korean frozen *bulgogi* and *kimchi* fried rice, and Whole Food Market (www.wholefoodsmarket.com) sells mixed grains, dried mushrooms, dried red chili peppers, and other products for the shoppers to conveniently choose by feature.

2 List of Alternative Food Ingredients Available in the Americas

Some vegetables including *doraji* (bellflower roots), *gosari* (bracken), *kong-namul* (bean sprouts), and green vegetables from mountains, Korean young/aged squash may be only available in Korean grocery stores and not in the local grocery stores. As vegetables that can be usually found in other countries may have different taste, you are recommended to first refer to the 'Alternative Food Materials' provided as a tip on the recipes.

Ssal (Rice) Short-grain rice is recommended for use in Korean cooking. Especially when making *gimbap* (toasted laver rolls) 70p, using short-grain rice that is stickier than long-grain rice helps to maintain the round shape of *gimbap* because the rice sticks together properly. However, it is acceptable to use long-grain rice which is easier to find in the Americas to make fried rice or *bibimbap* 52p. In addition, there are various types of pre-packaged cooked rice, and these are quite convenient. Pre-packaged rice is ready to eat after 2 minutes in the microwave.

Baechu (Napa cabbage) *Baechu* is called Chinese cabbage or Korean cabbage in the Americas. When it is difficult to find *baechu*, it is better to use bok choy than other cabbages.

Hobak (Squash) When there are no Korean young squash in the Americas, zucchini, which is green but less sweet than Korean young squash, may be used, or summer squashes such as yellow squash, which has a similar taste but is yellow, can also be substituted. For aged pumpkin, winter squashes such as acorn squash, butternut squash, pumpkin, or *dan-hobak* (kabocha squash) can be used instead.

Gochu (Chili pepper) Cayenne pepper is most similar to the *gochu* of Korea. However, it is fine to use poblano, anaheim, serrano, or jalapeno peppers, which have a different degree of spiciness.

Kkannip (Perilla leaf) *Kkannip* is the leaf of the perilla. It is similar to shiso leaf though its flavor is different.

Minari (Korean watercress) Korean watercress can be found in oriental Asian grocery stores. If it is difficult to obtain Korean watercress, it is acceptable to use western watercress instead although western watercress is more peppery than Korean watercress and thus different from the original flavor.

Buchu (Oriental chives) Oriental chives are sold in Asian grocery stores and are also called Oriental or Chinese chives. If oriental chives are difficult to find, regular chives can be found in the herb section of the grocery store. *Yeongyang* chives, which are a type of chives with extremely thin leaves that are eaten fresh in Korea, are quite similar to ordinary chives in grocery stores.

Jeok/Cheong Sangchu (Red/Green leaf lettuce) Leaf lettuce is widely used for wraps in Korea. Leaf vegetables such as romaine, iceberg lettuce, and other lettuces are all excellent for wraps instead of *jeok/cheong sangchu*. Additionally, leaf vegetables that have a bitter taste such as kale and mustard leaf are also good for wraps.

Kong-namul/Sukju (Bean sprouts/Mung bean sprouts) Though mung bean sprouts are easy to find, bean sprouts can only be found in Asian grocery stores. Most dishes that use bean sprouts can use mung bean sprouts although the bean sprouts taste will be missed when using mung bean sprouts.

Mu (White radish) Generally *mu* in the Americas refer to red radishes that are small and round ball-shaped. In Korean food, white, or oriental, daikon radishes are used. It may be difficult to distinguish oriental radishes from white radishes. However, they have similar textures and taste. White radishes are also used to make *kimchi* in Korea.

Doraji/Gosari (Bellflower roots/Bracken) Vegetables that are only eaten in Korea and are difficult to find in grocery stores. Dried bellflower roots and bracken are sold in Asian grocery stores and easy to find. These can be used after being soaked in water.

Oi (Cucumbers) Cucumbers in the Americas are thicker, have more seeds and thicker skins than ordinary Korean cucumbers. English cucumbers or hothouse cucumbers are most similar to Korean ones. Additionally, kirby cucumbers, which are smaller than 4-inch (10-cm) and are used for making pickles, have relatively fewer seeds and thinner skins.

Beoseot (Mushrooms) *Pyogo* (shiitake) mushrooms are the most commonly used mushrooms in Korean food, and it is convenient to have dried *pyogo* mushrooms stored in one's pantry. Button mushrooms do not have an extremely strong flavor and are easy to find. Therefore, they can be used in any mushroom dishes. Mushrooms such as portobello (popular and huge with an earthy flavor and meaty texture), porcini (with the most intense flavor), or cremini (also known as baby portobellos–with a more robust flavor and deeper color than button mushrooms) should be carefully selected because they have a strong flavor. Oyster mushrooms, king oyster mushrooms, and *paengi* (enoki) mushrooms have a mild flavor and, being easy to find in asian grocery stores, they can be used in any type of Korean food.

Bae (Korean pears) When eating fresh Korean pears, western pears cannot be substituted for Korean pears because their taste and texture are quite different. However, for food that uses ground pears for seasoning such as *bulgogi* (grilled maringted beef) 58p, western pears can be used instead although western pears are less sweet and less watery.

Yuja *Yuja* is in season only in November in Korea. *Yuja* tea is sold in Asian grocery stores. The tea looks like orange marmalade in a jar, and one can obtain preserved *yuja* from this.

Omija *Omija* is a type of berry that tastes similar to cranberries. *Omija* is sold in Asian grocery stores in a powder form or in the form of tea preserved in sugar. If cranberry juice or pomegranate juice is used instead of *omija*-infused water when making *omija* punch, the tastes are similar.

Daechu (Jujubes) *Jujubes* and dates are similar in shape, thus they are difficult to distinguish. Dates can be used instead of jujubes when making tea although dates cannot be used as a substitute for food that uses dried jujubes for garnish.

Yukryu (Meat) As unit of measure, packaging size differ in the Amricas compared to Korea, one must be aware and convert metric measurements into standard measurements, so marinades and seasonings are correctly portioned to the meat being prepared.

Saengseon (Fish) Cod, halibut, snapper, catfish, sea bass, sole, flounder, and tiliapia are the most commonly used white fleshed fish in Korea. And mackerel, sardines, herring, and swordfish are also commonly used as the blue colored fish. Also, salmon, trout, and tuna are popular as the red flesh fish.

Yangnyeom (Condiments)

As Korean traditional condiments, such as *ganjang* (soy sauce), *doenjang* (soybean paste), *gochu-jang* (red chili pepper paste), *chamgireum* (sesame oil), and *myeolchi-aekjeot* (fermented anchovy sauce) are what make Korean food taste truely Korean, you are recommended to buy Korean-made products. Even though other Asian countries' products are made from similar ingredients to ours, it may differ the taste due to the difference in processing. These products can be stored for a long time within your refrigerator. You can also conveniently purchase them from online markets, such as amazon.com.

Soguem (Salt) In Korea, two types of sea salt are most often used: *cheonilyeom* (natural sea salt; unrefined sea salt), and *kkot-soguem* (coarse sea salt; refined sea salt). Natural sea salt is used for brining *baechu* (napa cabbage) when making *kimchi* or salting fish. Coarse sea salt is used for seasoning food. Kosher salt can be used instead of coarse sea salt.

Ganjang (Soy sauce) It is better to use *ganjang* with a high salt content for soups and dark and a little sweet soy sauce for other Korean food. *Guk-ganjang* (soy sauce for soup) is saltier than *gangjang*, has a lighter color and is less sweet. One tablespoon of *guk-ganjang* can be substituted with 1 teaspoon of coarse sea salt and 1/4 teaspoon of *ganjang*.

Doenjang (Soybean paste) Sometimes *doenjang*, which has a higher content of beans than wheat, cannot be found, and only miso (Japanese-style soybean paste) is available. The miso that has a high wheat content and is sweet can be substituted with 1 tablespoon of miso mixed with 1 teaspoon of *ganjang* (soy sauce).

Gochu-jang (Red chili pepper paste) When there is no *gochu-jang*, a substitute can be made by mixing *doenjang* (soybean paste) and *gochut-garu*. In case *doenjang* is not available, *gochut-garu* can be used to create a spicy flavor, and *ganjang* (soy sauce) or salt can be used to season food. Hot sauce, such as Tabasco or Sriracha, that are easy to find in the Americas, are too sour and thus not suitable to be used instead of *gochu-jang*.

Gochut-garu (Red chili pepper powder) Instead of *gochut-garu*, cayenne pepper, which is similarly spicy and is easy to find, can be used. Powdered paprika pepper is similar to *gochut-garu* in color and scent. However, powdered paprika is sweet and does not have a spicy taste.

Sikcho (Vinegar) In Korea, brewed vinegars such as brown rice vinegar or apple vinegar are most often used. However, it is acceptable to use white vinegar, which is commonly found in the Americas.

Pa (Green onions) Green onions (or scallions) and thick green onions are most commonly used in Korea. It is difficult to find thick green onions in the Americas. Therefore, for soup that requires cooked thick green onions such as *yukgaejang* (spicy beef soup) 112p, leeks can be used instead. For foods other than soup that requires fresh thick green onions such as *kimchi*, green onions can be alternative. One stem of thick green onion equals 3 stems of green onions.

Gyeoja (Mustard) English mustard can be used instead of Korean mustard although English mustard has a less tang and a less spicy taste than Korean mustard. Powdered mustard and paste mustard in a tube are quite convenient. Both powdered and paste mustards are sold in Oriental grocery stores.

Myeolchi-aekjeot (Fermented anchovy sauce) Compared with Korean fish sauce such as *myeolchi aekjeot*, ordinary fish sauce generally contains seasonings other than simply fermented fish. Ordinary fish sauce is much sweeter than Korean fish sauce.

Kimchi As there are a variety of *kimchi* products available at the Asian grocery stores, you can conveniently purchase different types of *kimchi*, instead of making *kimchi* by yourself at home.

CHAPTER 3

Essential Ingredients for Korean Cuisine

These are the basic ingredients for Korean food. If you store these basic ingredients in your pantry, you can make Korean food anytime you want.

For the Cupboard

Ssal (rice): short-grain rice, *Milgaru* (all-purpose flour), *Sogeum* (salt) : *Cheonil-yeom* and *Kkot-soguem* (natural sea salt and coarse sea salt; Kosher salt can be substituted for sea salt), *Seoltang* (sugar), *Ganjang* (soy sauce), *Doenjang* (soybean paste), *Gochu-jang* (red chili pepper paste), *Chamgireum* (sesame oil), *Kkae-sogeum* (toasted and crushed sesame seeds), *Gochut-garu* (red chili pepper powder), *Huchu* (ground black pepper), *Sikcho* (vinegar), Vegetable oil

For the Fridge

Pa (green onion), *Maneul* (garlic), *Dubu* (tofu), *Kimchi* (fermented napa cabbage)

CHAPTER 4

Essential Korean Kitchenware

Generally, Korean foods are cooked on the stove top. It is not common to use ovens in Korean kitchens, but if you are familiar with oven cooking, you can use ovens for roasting or grilling meat dishes such as *Bulgogi* (Grilled marinated beef), *Galbi-gui* (Grilled beef short ribs), and *Neobiani* (Grilled marinated beef slices). One kind of all-purpose pot is sufficient for cooking, but the following kitchenwares are suggested to make various dishes more easily. The following lists include all of the equipment used in this book.

Pots and Pans

POT

Small (1-quart, 1L) pot : reheating small amounts of food
Medium (3-quart, 3L) pot : *bap* (cooked rice), *juk* (porridge), *guk/tang* (soups), *jjigae* (stews), blanching
Large (6-quart, 6L) pot : *guksu* (noodles), *gungmul* (broth), *jjim* (braised dishes)

PAN

Small (8-inch, 21-cm) frying pan : eggs
Medium (10-inch, 25-cm) frying pan : stir-fried dishes
Large (12-inch, 30-cm) frying pan : pan-fried dishes
Wok (12-inch, 30-cm) : deep-fried dishes, stir-fried dishes

Handy Kitchenware

Colander/Strainer (draining the soaked rice, cooked noodles, and blanched vegetables), Cutting board, Kitchen scissors, Paring knife (3-inch, 7~8-cm), Chef's knife (8-inch, 20~21-cm), Measuring cups (plastic metal, and/or pyrex) in 1/4 cup, 1/3 cup, 1/2 cup and 1 cup, Measuring spoons, Mixing bowls, Soup ladle, Wooden spoon, Turner

CHAPTER 5
Converting Measurements

Weight

Conventional measure	Metric Exact conversion measure grams (g)	Metric Approximate measure grams (g)
¼ oz.	7.1 grams	10 grams
½ oz.	14.2 grams	15 grams
1 oz.	28.3 grams	30 grams
2 oz.	56.7 grams	60 grams
3 oz.	85.0 grams	90 grams
3½ oz.	99.2 grams	100 grams
4 oz.	113.4 grams	120 grams
7 oz.	198.4 grams	200 grams
8 oz. (½ lb.)	226.8 grams	250 grams
10 oz.	283.9 grams	300 grams
16 oz. (1 lb.)	453.6 grams	500 grams
32 oz. (2 lb.)	907.2 grams	1 kilogram

Length

Conventional measure	Metric Exact conversion measure centimeters (cm)	Metric Approximate measure centimeters (cm)
1/16 inch	0.16 centimeter	0.15 centimeter
⅛ inch	0.32 centimeter	0.3 centimeter
½ inch	1.27 centimeters	1 centimeter
1 inch	2.54 centimeters	3 centimeters
1½ inches	3.81 centimeters	4 centimeters
2 inches	5.1 centimeters	5 centimeters

Volume

Conventional measure	Metric Exact conversion measure liter (L)	Metric Approximate measure liter (L)	Metric Approximate measure cups (C)
¼ quart	0.23 liter	¼ liter	1 cup
1 quart	0.93 liter	1 liter	4 cups
3 quarts	2.79 liters	3 liters	12 cups
4 quarts	3.72 liters	4 liters	16 cups
6 quarts	5.58 liters	6 liters	24 cups

CHAPTER 6
Basic Techniques

The following section looks into how to cut ingredients, cook rice, make broths, sauces and garnishes, which makes Korean dishes more beautiful.

1 Sseolgi (Cutting)

According to the types of ingredients and purpose of its use basic cutting fundamentally aims to cut ingredients in order to cook, eat and digest food easily while retaining the taste of food. By properly using various parts on the blade, practice cutting into even thickness, width and shape.

Slicing To slice is to cut the item into thin pieces as a whole or after cutting it into the desired length. Slicing is often used to make seasoned vegetables or stir-fry recipes.

Julienne To julienne is to cut the thinly sliced items into long thin strips. This is used to cut root vegetables for salads.

Mincing To mince is to gather julienned items neatly and cut into very small square pieces. This method is often used when preparing green onions, garlic, ginger, and onion for the sauce or marinade.

Batonnet To cut into batonnet is to cut the item into the proper length pieces and thick stick-shaped strips of the desired thickness.

Dice To dice is to cut radish, potato or *dubu* (tofu) into batonnet and then into cubes. This cutting method is often used to make *kkakdugi* (diced radish kimchi), *jorim* (braised dishes) or *jjigae* (stews).

Diagonal slicing Diagonal slicing is a method of cutting used to diagonally slice thin and long food items such as cucumber, carrot and spring onion, etc. into the desired thickness. This cutting method is suitable for *jorim* (braised dishes) because the ingredients have wider cross-sectional areas which the flavor can absorb.

Oblique cut/Roll cut This method is to cut thin and long food items such as cucumber and carrot into wedge-shaped pieces while turning the items round with one hand.

2 Bap (Cooked Rice)

In Korean cuisine, cooking rice is the most basic cooking method. The soaking time and water ratio differ according to the freshness and types of the rice and multi-grain. When cooking rice in a pot on the stove, the heat has to be adjusted from high to medium and finally to low heat. When cooking is done, turn off the heat and leave the pot covered for a while for more glutinous and tastier rice. These days, electric pressure cookers are popular, and these can easily reproduce the taste of rice cooked in a traditional iron pot. Instant cooked rice is also common, and it enables to have cooked rice in just 2 minutes in a microwave.

Cooking White Rice

The staple food for Koreans is cooked white rice. Cooked white rice, also called *baekban*, is cooked only with white short-grain without blending multi-grain.

Ingredients 2 cups short-grain rice (1 lb, 450g), 2 1/2 cups water (625ml)
Recipe
1 In a bowl, rinse the white rice several times by rubbing strongly until the water runs clear.
2 Depending on the weather and time of season, on average soak the rice in enough water for 30 minutes in summer or for 2 hours in winter, and drain in a colander.
3 Place the rice and 2 1/2 cups water in a heavy-bottom pot. Cover with a lid. Bring to a boil over high heat. Decrease the heat to medium and simmer gently for 4~5 minutes to prevent water from boiling over.
4 Reduce the heat to very low and simmer for 15 minutes. Increase the heat to high heat for 5 seconds to evaporate the extra water, and then remove the pot from the heat.
5 Leave the rice covered with a lid for 10~15 minutes, and fluff the rice with a wooden spoon.
Tip
A pot, pressure cooker, or an electric rice cooker is used, to cook rice.
A Pot When using a pot, the amount of water needed for cooking rice is 1.2 times the rice's volume or 1.3 times its weight. Because the volume of the rice increases during the cooking process, a pot at least 4 times higher than the height of the rice should be used, and it is better to choose a thick pot with a heavy lid.
A Pressure Cooker When using a pressure cooker, there is no need to presoak the rice, and the amount of water should be equal to the amount of rice. Although every rice cooker is different, start by setting the heat to a high level and then, either when the pressure pendulum moves and makes a sound or when the button on the lid acends one step, reduce the heat and boil the rice for 10~15 more minutes. Then turn off the heat and let the rice sit for 10 minutes.
An Electric Rice Cooker When using an electric rice cooker, measure the rice using the measuring cup that comes with the cooker, lay the rice flat in the pot and pour water up to the gradation markings inside the pot. Electric rice cookers have a warming function and keep the rice warm for approximately two days after cooking.

3 Gungmul (Broth)

With rice as the staple food, soup is a basic complimentary menu item that is served for every day meals. Broth is made from almost every ingredient, including meat, seafood and vegetables. The proper broth that goes well with the main ingredient will enrich the taste and flavor of the dish.

Beef Broth Deep and rich flavor of beef broth goes well with any Korean dishes. *Tteokguk* (sliced rice cake soup) 96p, *jeongol* (hot pots), *jjim* (steamed dishes) and even *doenjang-jjigae* (soybean paste stew) 106p taste better when boiled with beef broth.

Ingredients 1/2 lb (250g) beef brisket (or shank), 3 stalks leek (3 oz, 90g), 4 cloves garlic (2/3 oz, 20g), 9 cups water
Recipe
1 Soak the brisket in cold water for over an hour to remove blood.
2 In a large pot, put brisket, leeks, garlic, and cold water and bring to a boil. Reduce the heat to medium, cover a lid on, and simmer for an hour.
3 Skim off any impurities that rise to the surface while simmering.
4 Remove the pot from the heat and let it cool. Strain the broth through a sieve lined with cheesecloth and store in an airtight container in the refrigerator. Reserve the meat, and shred them into small pieces along the grain with hands or cut them across the grain with a knife.
Tip To use the meat in another dish, put the meat in boiling water. When using the meat to only make broth, put the meat in cold water and then start boiling.

Chicken Broth Chicken broth is used in Korea as well as in Western countries as it costs less while offering the unique taste of chicken.

Ingredients 1/2 chicken (1 lb, 500g), 3 stalks leek (3 oz, 90g), 4 cloves garlic (2/3 oz, 20g), 1 clove ginger (1/4 oz, 10g), 9 cups water, ground black pepper as needed
Recipe
1 Remove the fat attached to the chicken skin.
2 In a pot, bring enough water to a boil in order to blanch the chicken for a minute to remove the fat.
3 Pour off all the water and impurities and rinse the chicken with cold water. Return the chicken to the pot and add green onions, garlic, ginger, ground black pepper, and water. Bring to a boil over high heat. Reduce the heat to medium-low, cook for 40 minutes, and skim off any impurities that rise to the surface while boiling. Strain the broth through a sieve lined with cheesecloth and store in an airtight container in the refrigerator.
4 Put the chicken in a bowl to cool down. When the chicken is cool enough to handle, remove the bones and shred meat into small pieces along the grain with hands.
Tip When using fresh chicken or boneless chicken meat for the broth, parboiling is not necessary.

Anchovy Broth The flavor of anchovies brewed in a broth build the foundation of many dishes. It is widely used in the clear broth noodle soup, soup or stew flavored with *deonjang* (soybean paste), and/or *gochu-jang* (red chili pepper paste).

Ingredients 15 dried anchovies for broth (1/2 oz, 15g), 4 cups water
Recipe
1 Prepare the thick and shiny dried anchovies and remove the head and intestines.
2 In a skillet, stir-fry the anchovies for 3 minutes without vegetable oil over the medium heat to remove fishy odor.
3 Put the stir-fried anchovies in a pot. Pour the water into the pot and bring to a boil over high heat.
4 Reduce the heat to medium-low and simmer for 15 minutes. Then remove the anchovies from the broth.
Tip For additional flavor, brush off 2 sheets of thick 2x2-inch (5x5-cm) kelp with a clean wet cloth and soak in cold water for 30 minutes.

Vegetable Broth Clean and fresh taste from vegetables is suitable for making clear soup. It is popular due to the recent trend of well-being cuisines, weight loss, and incresed popularity of vegetarianism.

Ingredients 1/4 (16 oz, 500g) white radish, 1 (7 oz, 200g) onion, 3 dried *pyogo* (shiitake) mushrooms, 2X2-inch (5X5-cm) kelp, 10 cups water
Recipe
1 Cut the white radish and onion into quarters.
2 In a pot, put the white radish, onion, mushrooms, and kelp. Pour the water and bring to a boil.
3 When it gets to boil, remove the kelp from the pot and simmer for an hour over medium-low heat, covered. Strain the broth through a sieve lined with cheesecloth and store in an airtight container in the refrigerator.
Tip Leftover vegetables from cooking can be used for vegetable broth.

4 Yangnyeom-Jang (Marinades, Seasonings and Dipping Sauces)

In Korean cuisines, sauces can be largely categorized into meat marinades and seasoning sauces. These seasoning sauces have various usages such as dipping *jeon* (pan-fried dishes), pouring over *muk* (jellied food) and *saengchae* (salads) or *namul* (seasoned vegetables) to make *bibimbap*.

❶ Marinades and Seasonings

Meat marinade

This basic marinade goes well with any kind of ingredients including beef, pork and chicken, and it masks the unpleasant smell of fat from the meat. Marinades, seasoned with green onion, garlic, ginger and onion, can even tenderize the meat. A key flavoring step in this marinade is to add a proper amount of sugar or corn syrup to give a hint of sweetness.

Ganjang (Soy sauce) Marinade

Ingredients 5 tablespoons *ganjang* (soy sauce), 2 1/2 tablespoons sugar, 2 tablespoons chopped green onions, 1 tablespoon minced garlic, 1 tablespoon sesame oil, 1/2 tablespoon toasted sesame seeds, crushed, 1/2 teaspoon ground black pepper, salt as needed

Tip This is a suitable amount for 1 lb (500g) of meat added with a small amount of additional ingredients, such as onion, green onion and mushroom. It is recommended for *bulgogi* (grilled marinated beef) 58p, *neobiani* (grilled marinated beef slices) 118p and *galbi-gui* (grilled beef short ribs) 120p. When marinating short ribs with bones, this amount can marinate about 2 lb (1kg) of meat.

Spicy Marinade

Ingredients 2 tablespoons *gochut-garu* (red chili pepper powder), 3 tablespoons *gochu-jang* (red chili pepper paste), 2 tablespoons *ganjang* (soy sauce), 1 tablespoon sugar, 2 tablespoons corn syrup, 2 tablespoons rice wine, 2 tablespoons chopped green onions, 1 tablespoon minced garlic, 1 teaspoon minced ginger, 1 tablespoon sesame oil, 1/2 tablespoon toasted sesame seeds, crushed, 1/2 teaspoon ground black pepper

Tip This can marinate about 1 lb (500g) of pork or chicken. This spicy marinade is recommended for braised or stir-fried meat. When boned chicken is used, it can marinate 2 lb (1kg) of meat.

Seasoning for Braising

This marinade is recommended for braising *dubu* (tofu), potatoes or dried anchovies. It is better to boil the marinade in advance. The secret of flavoring is to add fresh green chili peppers or *geon-gochu* (dried red chili peppers) to spice up the taste.

Sweet Braising Seasoning

Ingredients 1/2 cup *ganjang* (soy sauce), 1 tablespoon sugar, 2 tablespoons corn syrup, 1 tablespoon rice wine, 1 tablespoon minced garlic, 1/2 teaspoon ginger juice, 2 *geon-gochu* (dried red chili peppers), 1 cup water

Tip This marinade is used to cook clean and non-spicy dish from dried seafood such as dried anchovies. It can be also used to make braised potatoes or fishes.

Spicy Braising Seasoning
Ingredients 3 tablespoons *ganjang* (soy sauce), 1/2 tablespoon sugar, 1/2 tablespoon *gochut-garu* (red chili pepper powder), 1 tablespoon chopped green onion, 1 teaspoon minced garlic, 1 teaspoon toasted sesame seeds, crushed, 1 teaspoon sesame oil
Tip It goes well with braised fish 148p or *dubu* (tofu).

Seasoning for Namul
This goes well with popular *namul* (seasoned vegetables) dishes such as spinach, bean sprouts and eggplants and with spicy dishes of squid and whelk. The secret of flavoring is to mix it right before serving rather than preparing in advance.

Namul Seasoning Flavored with *Guk-ganjang* (Soy sauce for soup)
Ingredients 1 1/2 tablespoons *guk-ganjang*, 1 tablespoon sugar, 1 tablespoon minced green onion, 1/2 tablespoon minced garlic, 1/2 tablespoon sesame oil, pinch of toasted sesame seeds, crushed
Tip This seasoning is flavored with *guk-ganjang*, which has lighter color and less sweet taste. This is proper amount for 10 oz (300g) of vegetables, and it can be used to stir-fry or season the bracken or spinach.

Spicy Seasoning
Ingredients 2 tablespoons *gochut-garu* (red chili pepper powder), 1 tablespoon *gochu-jang* (red chili pepper paste), 1 tablespoon *ganjang* (soy sauce), 2 tablespoons vinegar, 1 tablespoon sugar, 2 tablespoons corn syrup , 1 tablespoon chopped green onion, 1/2 tablespoon minced garlic, 1/2 tablespoon sesame oil, 1 teaspoon toasted sesame seeds, crushed, salt as needed
Tip This sauce has spicy taste with sweet and sour flavor to it. It is a good sauce when mixing parboiled squid, whelk, cucumber or soaked seaweed. For 10 oz (300g) of the main ingredient, this is the right amount of seasoning.

Geot-jeori and Kimchi Seasoning
These are seasonings for *kimchi* and for *geot-jeori* that can be instantly made by mixing it with lightly salted napa cabbage, lettuce or julienned white radish. This amount is suitable to season 10 oz (300g) of the main ingredient.

Geot-jeori (Fresh kimchi) Seasoning
Ingredients 1/2 cup *gochut-garu* (red chili pepper powder), 2 tablespoons *ganjang* (soy sauce), 1 cup water, 2 tablespoons chopped green onion, 1 teaspoon minced ginger, 1 tablespoon toasted sesame seeds, 1 tablespoon sesame oil, 1 tablespoon sugar, 1 tablespoon salted shrimp, pinch of salt
Tip This seasoning is used to mix lettuce, heart of napa cabbage, cucumber or Korean chives. When mixing cucumber to serve immediately, add a small amount of vinegar to give a refreshing taste.

Kimchi Seasoning
Ingredients 10 cups *gochut-garu* (red chili pepper powder), 10 cloves garlic, minced, 3 cloves ginger, minced, 1/2 stalk leek, 1 cup salted shrimps, 1 cup anchovy sauce, 1/2 cup sugar, salt as needed
Tip It is suitable to season 10 whole napa cabbages. Minor ingredients other than basic seasoning such as oysters and shrimps can be used according to taste.

❷ Dipping Sauce

Cho-ganjang (Soy sauce with vinegar)
This sauce is mainly made of soy sauce and vinegar. Its sour taste stimulates the appetite, and it is also easy to make.

Ingredients 1 tablespoon *ganjang* (soy sauce), 1 tablespoon water, 1 teaspoon sugar, 1 tablespoon vinegar, 1/2 teaspoon ground pine nuts (optional for garnish)
Tip Mix soy sauce, water, sugar and vinegar, and serve with ground pine nuts on top.

Cho-gochu-jang (Red chili pepper paste with vinegar)
This spicy and sour red chili pepper paste sauce suits foreigners' tastes. In addition to dipping raw fish, fresh seaweed or fresh oysters, it can be used to make fresh tasting *bibimbap* by mixing fresh vegetables and rice.

Ingredients 4 tablespoons *gochu-jang* (red chili pepper paste), 1/2 tablespoon *ganjang* (soy sauce), 1/2 tablespoon rice wine, 3 tablespoons vinegar, 2 tablespoons sugar, 2 teaspoons garlic juice, 1/2 teaspoon ginger juice, 2 tablespoons water, pinch of gound pine nuts (optional)
Tip Generally, white vinegar is used, though the different types of vinegar can be used for more unique flavors.

Gyeoja-jang (Mustard sauce)
It is deliciously flavored with a hint of sourness and distinctive pungent taste of mustard.
Ingredients 2 tablespoons hot mustard powder, 3 tablespoons water, 1/2 teaspoon *ganjang* (soy sauce), 1/2 teaspoon salt, 1 tablespoon sugar, 1 tablespoon vinegar
Recipe
1 Place mustard powder in a bowl and add 2 tablespoons of water. Mix well and let stand in a warm place.
2 When it turns dark, dries and cracks, pour an additional 1/2 cup of hot water carefully. Set aside to remove the astringency, and then drain off water.
3 Add 1 tablespoon of water, soy sauce, salt, sugar, and vinegar and mix well without lumps.
Tip Instead of soaking mustard powder before use, premixed mustard in tubes sold at the market can be used.

Ssam-jang (Seasoned soybean paste)
Seasoned soybean paste is used to dip lettuce or cabbage wrappers with grilled meat. This sauce is nice and salty with nutty flavor.

Ingredients 2 oz (50g) ground beef, 2 dried *pyogo* (shiitake) mushrooms, 1 green chili pepper, 4 tablespoons *doenjang* (soybean paste), 2 teaspoons *gochu-jang* (red chili pepper paste), 1 tablespoon chopped green onion, 1/2 tablespoon minced garlic, 1/2 cup water, 1 tablespoon sesame oil
Recipe
1 Soak the *pyogo* mushrooms in cold water and cut into fine julienne. Cut the green chili pepper in half lengthwise and remove seeds. Slice the pepper diagonally and thinly.
2 In a skillet, put the ground beef, mushrooms, *doenjang*, *gochu-jang*, minced green onion, minced garlic, and water and mix well. Bring to a boil, then reduce the heat to low and simmer.
3 When it turns thick, add green chili pepper and sesame oil and cook for an additional 5 minutes.
Tip Depending on the saltiness of *doenjang*, the taste of *ssam-jang* may differ.

Yak-gochu-jang (Seasoned red chili pepper paste)

Seasoned red chili pepper paste is made of minced beef, honey, and sesame oil. The flavor of the sauce is spicy and sweet and it captures your palette. It is served with lettuce wrappers and *bibimbap*.

Ingredients 1 1/2oz (50g) ground beef, marinade for beef (1/2 tablespoon *ganjang* (soy sauce), 1 tablespoon sugar, 1 teaspoon sesame oil, pinch of ground black pepper), 1/2 lb (250g) *gochu-jang* (red chili pepper paste), 2 tablespoons water, 2 tablespoons honey, 2 tablespoons sesame oil, 1 tablespoon pine nuts (optional)

Recipe
1 Marinate ground beef with soy sauce, sugar, sesame oil, and ground black pepper. Heat a skillet over medium high heat, stir-fry the beef and set aside. Chop them finely when cooled.
2 In a pot, put stir-fried beef, *gochu-jang*, and water and mix well. Bring to a boil, then lower the heat and simmer, stirring with a wooden spoon.
3 When *gochu-jang* starts to get darker, add honey and sesame oil and continue cooking by stirring.
4 When it turns dark, thick, and shiny, remove from the heat and mix with pine nuts. Let it cool.

5 Gomyeong (Garnish)

Gyeran-jidan (Yellow and White egg garnish)

Ingredients 1 egg, pinch of salt, vegetable oil as needed
Recipe
1 Separate egg yolks and egg whites into two bowls.
2 Sprinkle pinch of salt to each bowl and beat well, respectively, to break the chalazae. Skim off any foam that rises to the surface and set aside.
3 Heat a skillet. Apply vegetable oil to a paper towel and coat the bottom of a pan.
4 Reduce heat to low, then pour and fry each of the egg mixtures into thin layers, respectively.
5 Set aside to let them cool. Cut them into a very fine julienne strips, 1x1.5-inch (2.5 x 3.5-cm)-sized squares or diamonds shapes depending on dishes.

Silkkae (Toasted peeled sesame seeds)

Ingredients 1 cup sesame seeds
Recipe
1 Wash the sesame seeds and soak in water for over 3 hours.
2 Grind soaked sesame seeds in a food processor with water until skins come off.
3 Transfer to a bowl and pour enough water into. Rub with hands and leave remained skins until skins float to the surface.
4 Remove floating skins. Repeat the process of pouring water and removing floating skins until the skins don't come to the surface.
5 Place the sesame seeds in a fine sieve and drain. Toast the sesame seeds in a pan over the high heat until the water evaporates. Reduce the heat to low and toast until the sesame seeds are fully swelled.
6 Pass the toasted sesame through a fine sieve into a bowl and discard the residue.

Tip Toasted sesame seeds can be purchased at an Asian grocery stores.

Beoseot (Mushroom) Garnish

Ingredients dried *pyogo* (shiitake) mushrooms, cold water
dried *seogi* (stone) mushrooms, boiling water
dried *mogi* (wood ear) mushrooms, cold water

Recipe

Pyogo mushrooms

1 Soak the dried *pyogo* mushrooms in cold water sufficiently for approximately 5 hours depending on the dried states. It should be soaked until the white and hard-core is softened. It will take a long time to be fully soaked so prepare prior to making other foods. You may soak the mushrooms in boiling water if the ingredient is needed urgently, but a large amount of savory components will come out. When *pyogo* mushrooms of 1/4 oz (10g) are soaked, they become 1 oz (30g).
2 Squeeze out excess water and cut into fine julienne.
3 Season mushrooms with soy sauce.
4 Heat a small amount of oil in a skillet and stir-fry seasoned mushroom quickly.

Seogi mushrooms

1 Soak the dried *seogi* mushrooms in boiling water. Remove the slippery mosses inside of mushrooms by rubbing with hands and eliminate the foreign debris. When 1/4 oz (10g) of dried *seogi* mushrooms are soaked, it becomes about 2 oz (60g).
2 Overlap the soaked pieces of mushrooms and roll them into a tight cylinder and slice crosswise into thin shreds.
3 Heat a small amount of oil in a skillet. Add a little of salt and sesame oil and stir-fry mushrooms quickly.

Mogi mushrooms

1 Soak the dried *mogi* mushrooms in cold water for 30 minutes. When 1/4 oz (10g) of dried *mogi* mushrooms are soaked, it becomes about 2 oz (60g).
2 Squeeze out excess water and tear each mushroom.
3 Season mushrooms with soy sauce.
4 Heat a small amount of oil in a skillet and stir-fry seasoned *mogi* mushrooms quickly.

Top 12 Korean Food

Rice Mixed with Vegetables and Beef
Bibimbap 비빔밥

> Bibimbap is a dish made up of various seasoned vegetables and meat and eaten after mixing all of the ingredients with *gochu-jang* (red chili pepper paste). For better taste, use various in-season vegetables and add sesame oil. Because it contains various types of vegetables, one bowl of *bibimbap* can be a nutritionally balanced meal.
>
> It is said that in traditional Korean palaces, *bibimbap* was called '*bibim*' or '*goldongban*' and was eaten on the last day of the year (December 31).

Serves 4

4 bowls cooked white rice (2 lb, 920g 78p)
gochu-jang (red chili pepper paste), sesame oil as needed

Seasoned mushrooms
5 fresh *pyogo* (shiitake) mushrooms (5 oz, 150g) (or oyster mushrooms)
pinch of salt, 1 teaspoon vegetable oil

Seasoned spinach
5 oz (150g) fresh spinach
pinch of salt, 2 teaspoons soy sauce, 1 teaspoon sesame oil, ½ teaspoon toasted sesame seeds, crushed

Seasoned bean sprouts
5 oz (150g) fresh bean sprouts
pinch of salt
½ tablespoon sesame oil

Marinade for beef
5 oz (150g) ground beef
1 tablespoon soy sauce,
½ tablespoon sugar,
2 teaspoons minced green onion, 1 teaspoon minced garlic, 2 teaspoons sesame oil, 2 teaspoons toasted sesame seeds, crushed, pinch of ground black pepper

Preparation

1 Remove the stems of *pyogo* mushrooms. Cut the mushrooms into ⅛×⅛×2-inch (0.3×0.3×5-cm) julienne strips.
2 Rinse the spinach and bean sprouts thoroughly.
3 Combine all the ingredients of the marinade for the beef in a small bowl. Add the ground beef to the bowl and marinate for 5 minutes.

Cooking

1 Place a skillet over medium heat. Add the vegetable oil and stir-fry the *pyogo* mushrooms with a pinch of salt.
2 In a medium saucepan, boil 3 cups of water and blanch the spinach for 1 minute with a pinch of salt. Rinse immediately with cold water and squeeze out the excess water from the spinach. Cut in half if necessary, then season the spinach with salt, soy sauce, sesame oil and crushed sesame seeds.
3 In a medium saucepan, put the bean sprouts and add water and a pinch of salt. Cover the saucepan and bring to a boil. Reduce the heat to low and cook for 15 minutes until the beans are cooked. Remove and season the bean sprouts with salt and sesame oil.
4 Place a skillet over high heat and stir-fry the marinated beef.
5 Place a scoop of cooked rice in the individual bowl and arrange the *pyogo* mushroom, spinach, bean sprouts and beef side by side on top of the rice.
6 Serve the *gochu-jang* and sesame oil on the side.

Tip

Any vegetables can be used for *bibimbap*. Generally, three or more types of in-season vegetables are used. Green vegetables include cucumbers, zucchini, spinach 164p, Korean watercress and crown daisy. White vegetables include bellflower roots 166p, mung bean sprouts, bean sprouts 164p and radishes. Brown vegetables include bracken 166p and *pyogo* (shiittake) mushrooms 164p.
Dolsot-bibimbap is *bibimbap* cooked in a hot stone pot. It is cooked by placing rice and vegetables into a greased stone pot that retains its heat until the meal is finished. If a Korean stone pot is unavailable, a thickly lined cast-iron skillet or an oven-safe casserole may be used.

Spicy Soft Dubu Stew
Sundubu-jjigae 순두부찌개

> This spicy dish is made by boiling soft *dubu* (tofu), beef, seafoods and vegetables in a meat broth in a stone pot; sometimes, eggs are used. The soup may be boiled clear, or it may be spiced with *gochut-garu* (red chili pepper powder).
> *Dubu* is one of the most popular ingredients in Korean dishes. Although *dubu* has traditionally been popular in Eastern countries, it recently has become popular in the other countries, too.

Serves 4

1 lb (500g) soft *dubu* (tofu)
3½ oz (100g) ground pork
3½ oz (100g) oyster mushrooms
1 tablespoon vegetable oil
3½ cups water
pinch of salt
4 eggs

Spicy seasoning
1 tablespoon *gochut-garu* (red chili pepper powder),
1 tablespoon sesame oil,
1 tablespoon minced green onion, 1 teaspoon minced garlic, 1 tablespoon soy sauce for soup, 2 tablespoons water

Preparation

1. Drain the soft *dubu* in a colander and break into large pieces.
2. Shred the oyster mushrooms into thin strips.
3. Mix *gochut-garu* well with sesame oil, and then combine with the minced green onion, minced garlic, soy sauce for soup, and water to make the spicy seasoning.

Cooking

1. Heat a medium saucepan over medium heat and add the vegetable oil. Stir-fry the ground pork with the spicy seasoning.
2. When the pork is cooked, pour 3½ cups of water and bring to a boil. When it boils, add the soft *dubu* and oyster mushrooms and reduce the heat to low. Simmer for 10 minutes and season to taste with salt.
3. Divide the stew into 4 small individual saucepans and add the egg in each saucepan. Bring to a boil until the egg white is cooked. You could also cook the stew in a large saucepan; add the beaten eggs over the stew before serving. Ladle into the individual bowls.

Tip

There are many types of *dubu*. *Sun-dubu* (soft *dubu*) 31p is made by coagulating soymilk protein without draining the water. Soft *dubu* is known for its characteristic soft taste. If soft *dubu* is unavailable, *yeon-dubu* (silk *dubu*) 31p is recommended over firm *dubu*.
Soft *dubu* is readily available in Asian grocery stores, and it is traditionally in a long tubed shaped container.

P1
P2
P3
C1
C2

Dumplings
Mandu 만두

> The dumplings are made by filling meat and vegetables into thinly kneaded flour dough wrapper. In autumn and winter, dumplings with meat, *dubu* (tofu) and *kimchi* fillings are the best; steamed dumplings with finely julienned cucumbers, meat and *pyogo* (shiitake) mushrooms are the best in summer.

Serves 4

Wrappers
12 oz (360g) all-purpose flour
1½ cups water
1 teaspoon salt
½ cup flour for dusting or store-bought dumpling wrappers (about 50 to a package)

Filling
5 oz (150g) ground beef
1 package firm *dubu* (tofu) (10 oz, 300g)
7 oz (200g) mung bean sprouts
3½ oz (100g) Korean chives
2 tablespoons minced green onion, 1 tablespoon sesame oil, 1 teaspoon salt, ground black pepper as needed

Marinade for beef
1 teaspoon soy sauce,
1 teaspoon salt, 1 teaspoon minced garlic, ground black pepper as needed

Cho-ganjang (Soy sauce with vinegar)
2 tablespoons soy sauce,
2 tablespoons white vinegar,
1 tablespoon water,
1 teaspoon *gochut-garu* (red chili pepper powder)

Tip

Dumpling types vary depending on wrapper and filling ingredients, their shape, and cooking method.
The thinner the dumpling wrappers, the better the dumplings taste.
Finished dumplings may be boiled in water, steamed, pan-fried in an oiled pan or boiled in broth.
Dumpling wrappers are available in grocery stores, and Asian grocery stores sell various types of frozen dumplings. Thin round dumpling wrappers taste better than spring rolls or egg rolls.
Western chives can be used in Korean chives are unavailable.

Preparation

If using store bought dumpling wrappers, omit step **1** and **2**.

1. In a large bowl, mix the flour, salt and water. Knead the dough until soft and smooth. Place the dough in a plastic bag and rest it for 30 minutes.
2. Sprinkle the dusting flour onto a work surface. Roll out the dough until ⅛-inch (0.3-mm) thick. Cut out the dough with a 3-inch (8-cm) diameter round mold. Dust the flour between the wrappers so they will not stick together.
3. In a small bowl, season the ground beef with the soy sauce, salt, garlic and ground black pepper.
4. Wrap the *dubu* in cheesecloth or paper towels. Squeeze out as much liquid as possible.
5. Rinse the bean sprouts and then parboil them in the boiling water with salt. They will appear translucent. Squeeze out the excess water and mince.
6. Trim the end of the Korean chives off and then mince them finely.
7. In a small bowl, combine all the ingredients of the *cho-ganjang* for dipping.

Cooking

1. To make the filling, in a large bowl, combine the ground beef, *dubu*, bean sprouts, Korean chives, green onions, garlic, sesame oil, salt and ground black pepper. Mix well.
2. Place a wrapper in your palm. Dab some water around the edge of the wrapper with your finger. Place a generous tablespoonful of filling on the center of the wrapper. Fold the wrapper into a half-moon, then pinch edges to seal, eliminating any air inside. You may shape the dumplings in various shapes making sure the edges are sealed.
3. Steam the dumplings in a steamer for 20 minutes.
4. Serve the dumplings with a small bowl of *cho-ganjang*.

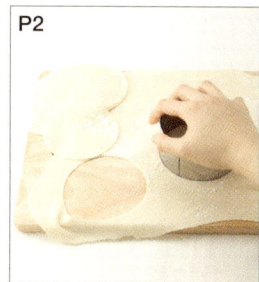

Grilled Marinated Beef
Bulgogi 불고기

" *Bulgogi* is a signature Korean meat dish made by marinating thinly sliced beef in soy sauce and then grilling it. Although the name *bulgogi* means meat grilled on fire, *bulgogi* is generally stir-fried in a moist pan. "

Serves 4

1 lb (500g) beef (sirloin)
1 onion (7 oz, 200g)
3 *pyogo* (shiitake) mushrooms (or oyster mushrooms) (3 oz, 90g)
6 stalks green onion (2 oz, 60g)
1 tablespoon vegetable oil

Marinade for beef
5 tablespoons soy sauce,
3 tablespoons sugar,
2 tablespoons minced green onion, 1 tablespoon minced garlic, 1 tablespoon sesame oil, ½ teaspoon ground black pepper, 1 tablespoon toasted sesame seeds, crushed

*optional for marinade
¼ Korean pear (5 oz,150g, 5 tablespoons pear juice) or
5 tablespoons beef broth
2 tablespoons rice wine

Preparation

1 Cut the beef into thin slices 1/10-inch (2-mm) thick across the grain, or have butcher slice meat for you. If necessary, cut into smaller bite-size pieces. Pat meat dry with paper towels to remove excess blood.
2 Cut onion into long thin slices.
3 Cut the mushrooms into thin slices.
4 Slice the green onions into 1½-inch (4-cm) long pieces.
5 Grate the pear and combine with all ingredients of the marinade for beef and mix well in a big bowl.
6 Add the beef to the marinade and toss meat so marinade coats all of the meat. Let it stand about 20 minutes. Add onion, green onions and mushrooms and mix well.

Cooking

1 Pan fry the beef in a small amount of oil until tender over the high heat. You may grill the meat over an open fire or grill.

Tip

In general, *bulgogi* is made from rib-eye sirloin, tenderloin or strip loin.
The thinner the meat, the better the marination. To thinly slice the meat, leave it in a freezer for 30 minutes and slice in the opposite direction of the grain using a sharp blade.
Add fruits, such as pears or apples, to the marinade sauce to make the meat more tender and for a sweet flavor.
Skewer the marinated meat and vegetables to make '*sanjeok*'. Alternate the meat with green onions and mushrooms for a more beautiful color and better taste.
Although it is common in Korean homes to cook *bulgogi*, *neobiani* (grilled marinated beef slices) 118p and *galbi-gui* (grilled beef short ribs) 120p in a frying pan, ovens may be used in places where ovens are more common. Grilling on a direct flame results in a better taste, due to the smoke; however, it is recommended to barbeque on a charcoal fire outside, not inside.

P1

P2 » P4

P5

P6

C1

Braised Short Ribs in Soy Sauce
Galbi-jjim 갈비찜

> *Galbi-jjim* is a dish made by steaming beef (or pork) ribs, radishes, carrots, chestnuts and jujube in soy sauce. *Galbi-jjim* is one of the signature dishes of the Korean New Year and *Chuseok*, which are traditional Korean holidays. Because of Koreans' preference for beef over any other meat, this dish is popular when welcoming visitors.

Serves 4

2 lb (1kg) beef short ribs with bones (2-inch (5-cm) long)
5 cups water
2 cups reserved beef broth
⅛ white radish (½ lb, 250g)
½ carrot (3½ oz, 100g)
6 dried *pyogo* (shiitake) mushrooms (1 oz, 30g) after soaking (3 oz, 90g)
5 chestnuts
3 jujubes
vegetable oil, salt as needed

Seasoning for beef
4 tablespoons soy sauce,
4 tablespoons pear juice (or 4 tablespoons water, 1 tablespoon sugar),
2 tablespoons sugar,
2 tablespoons minced green onion,
1 tablespoon minced garlic,
1 tablespoon sesame oil,
1 tablespoon toasted sesame seeds, crushed,
pinch of ground black pepper

Preparation

1 Cut the white radish and carrot into 1½-inch (4-cm) cubes, and round the edges.
2 Soak the *pyogo* mushrooms in water and strain. Once soaked, remove the stems.
3 Peel the chestnuts and remove the seed from jujubes.
4 Combine all the ingredients of the marinade for beef.

Cooking

1 Place the ribs in a pot and cover with cold water to remove any blood from the ribs. Drain the ribs in a colander and discard the water. Pour 5 cups of water into a pot and bring to a boil. When it boils, add the ribs and cook for 30 minutes. Skim off foam several times. Remove the ribs to a platter and set aside until they're cool enough to handle. Reserve the broth in the pot. Remove the extra fat and score diagonally 1-inch (3-cm) intervals.
2 Let the broth cool and skim off the fat.
3 In a medium saucepan, pour the water and bring to a boil. Add the white radish and carrots and parboil for 10 minutes. Remove and set aside.
4 In a pot, place the prepared short ribs and pour ⅔ part of the marinade and mix well. Add the 2 cups of reserved broth and bring to a boil for about 40 minutes over medium heat.
5 When the ribs become tender, add the parboiled white radish, carrots, *pyogo* mushrooms, chestnuts, jujubes and the rest of marinade. Reduce the heat to a simmer, and cook for an additional 15 minutes.
6 Arrange the ribs and vegetables in a serving bowl.

Tip

Beef shank, brisket or oxtail may be used instead of ribs.
Let the boiled ribs cool and separate the fat before cooking them with sauce to prevent excessive greasiness.

P1

C1

C4

C5

Spicy Stir-fried Pork
Dwaeji-bulgogi _Jeyuk-bokkeum

돼지불고기 _제육볶음

> " This dish is made by marinating thinly sliced pork in a *gochu-jang* (red chili pepper paste) sauce.
> It is more commonly known as '*jeyuk-bokkeum*,' and it is one of the most popular dishes in Korea. "

Serves 4

1 lb (500g) pork (belly)
1¼ onions (½ lb, 250g)
9 stalks green onion (3 oz, 90g)
2 tablespoons vegetable oil
Spicy marinade for pork
4 tablespoons *gochu-jang* (red chili pepper paste),
2 tablespoons *gochut-garu* (red chili pepper powder),
2 tablespoons soy sauce,
2 tablespoons sugar,
2 teaspoons minced green onion, 1 teaspoon minced garlic, 1 tablespoon ginger juice, 2 tablespoons rice wine, pinch of ground black pepper

Preparation

1. Slice the pork into ⅛-inch (0.3-cm) thick and cut into bite sizes.
2. Cut the onion into julienne lengthwise.
3. Slice the 6 stalks green onion into 1½-inch (4-cm) long pieces and chop the remaining green onions for garnish.
4. Combine *gochu-jang* and other ingredients of the spicy marinate for pork in a medium bowl.
5. Toss the pork in the marinade to coat and set aside for 30 minutes.

Cooking

1. In a skillet, heat the 1 tablespoon of vegetable oil. Stir-fry the sliced onion and set aside.
2. Heat the remaining 1 tablespoon of vegetable oil over medium heat. Add the pork and cook, stirring occasionally to avoid burning. When the pork is cooked thoroughly, add the stir-fried onion and toss.
3. Place the pork in a serving plate and garnish with the chopped green onions.

Tip

The spicy *gochu-jang* sauce used to marinate the meat is more suitable for pork than it is for beef.
Fatty pork belly cuts taste best. If lean shoulder or tenderloin is used, cut it into thin slices for a soft texture.
An alternative to pork, chicken can be grilled and marinated in the *gochu-jang* sauce. Onions, carrots, perilla leaves and cabbage may be stir-fried together according to the diner's preference.

P1

P2 » P3

P5

C2

Assorted Savory Pancakes
Modum-jeon 모둠전

> This dish is prepared by placing colorful savory pancakes made by pan-frying flour with egg-covered meat, fish and vegetables.
> *Modum-jeon* made of *ae-hobak-jeon* (pan-fried Korean young squash), *saengseon-jeon* (pan-fried white fish fillet) and *gogi-jeon* (pan-fried beef cakes).

Serves 4

Pan-fried Korean young squash
1 Korean young squash (10 oz, 300g)
⅓ cup all-purpose flour
2 eggs
salt, vegetables oil as needed

Pan-fried fish fillets
8 oz (250g) cod fillets (or any white fishes such as the croaker, pollack, sole, etc.)
salt, ground black pepper as needed
⅓ cup all-purpose flour
2 eggs
vegetable oil as needed

Pan-fried beef cakes
7 oz (200g) ground beef (top round)
⅓ package firm *dubu* (tofu) (3½ oz, 100g)
½ cup all-purpose flour, 2 eggs, vegetable oil as needed

Marinade for beef
2 teaspoons salt, ½ teaspoon sugar, 1 tablespoon minced green onion, 1 teaspoon minced garlic, 1 teaspoon sesame oil, 2 teaspoons toasted sesame seeds, crushed, ¼ teaspoon ground black pepper

Cho-ganjang (Soy sauce with vinegar)
2 tablespoons soy sauce,
1 tablespoon water,
1 tablespoon white vinegar,
½ teaspoon pine nuts, ground (optional)

Preparation

1 Slice Korean young squash crosswise into ¼-inch (0.5-cm) thick rounds. Season lightly with salt.
2 Slice the white fish fillet into bite-sized pieces.
3 Wrap the *dubu* in clean cheesecloth and squeeze out as much water as possible. Using a fork, finely mash it.
4 In a large bowl, combine the ground beef and mashed *dubu*. Add all the ingredients of the marinade and mix well. Shape into flat cakes, about 1~2-inch (3~5-cm) in diameter and ½-inch (1-cm) thick.
5 Beat eggs well in a bowl.
6 Combine all the ingredients to make *cho-ganjang* for dipping.

Cooking

Ae-hobak-jeon (Pan-fried Korean young squash)
1 Pat dry the seasoned squash with a paper towel to remove exess water.
2 Heat a skillet over medium heat and add vegetable oil. Dredge the squash with flour and then dip into beaten eggs to lightly coat. Pan-fry slowly in a small amount of oil until golden brown on both sides.
3 Serve with *cho-ganjang*.

Saengseon-jeon (Pan-fried fish fillets)
1 Sprinkle salt and ground black pepper on fish fillets.
2 Heat a pan over medium heat and add vegetable oil. Dredge the fish fillets with flour, and then dip into beaten eggs to lightly coat. Pan-fry slowly in a small amount of oil until golden brown on both sides.
3 Serve with *cho-ganjang*.

Gogi-jeon (Pan-fried beef cakes)
1 Heat a skillet over medium heat and add vegetable oil. Dredge the beef cakes with flour, then dip into beaten eggs to lightly coat. Pan-fry slowly in a small amount of oil until golden brown on both sides.
2 Serve with *cho-ganjang*.

Tip

Ingredients for savory pancakes include vegetables such as zucchini, sweet potato, *saesongi* (king oyster) mushrooms and *pyogo* (shiitake) mushrooms, white fish such as cod, croaker and frozen pollack and seafood such as shrimp and oysters. For meat pancakes, beef and pork may be used.
There are two types of meat pancakes. One is *yuk-jeon*, which is made from sliced meat, and the other is *gogi-jeon*, which is made from meatballs with added *dubu* (tofu) seasoned with various spices. *Dubu* in *gogi-jeon* adds moisture and texture.

P1
P2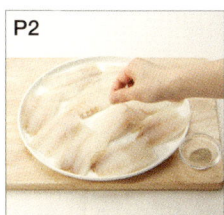
P4
C2
C2

Seafood and Green Onion Pancake
Haemul-pajeon 해물파전

> This dish is made by pan-frying flour batter with julienned spring onions, squid, clam meat and oysters.
> *Haemul-pajeon* is served with a *cho-ganjang* (soy sauce with vinegar) for dipping. Although green onions are popular for sauces, there are few recipes that feature green onions as the main ingredients. *Haemul-pajeon* with a generous amount of seafood and green onions is popular and is an ideal as a snack or with relish.

Serves 4

Makes 4 sheets
10 stalks green onion (3½ oz, 100g)
1½ oz (45g) Korean chives
4 oz (120g) clam meat
4 oz (120g) oysters
4 oz (120g) squid
vegetable oil as needed

Batter
2 cups all-purpose flour
2 cups water
3 eggs
½ tablespoon salt

Cho-ganjang (Soy sauce vinegar)
2 tablespoons soy sauce,
1 tablespoon white vinegar,
½ tablespoon sugar,
1 tablespoon water,
1 teaspoon *gochut-garu* (red chili pepper powder) (optional)

Tip

The flour or rice flour batter should be very watery. Include the batter only to the extent that it holds the ingredients together and pan-fry it until it is golden.

For a crispier *haemul-pajeon*, use a prepackaged savory pancake mix or prepackaged frying mix instead of flour or rice flour.

Parboil the seafood before mixing it to remove the moisture from the *pajeon*. That way, you can enjoy a more crispy texture.

A thin layer of batter in the pan to form a pancake, then the vegetables, seafood and other ingredients can be placed on top.

Once the pancake is half cooked place the egg on top of the vegetable seafood side, then filp. Cook until both sides are golden brown.

Preparation

1. Cut the green onions and Korean chives into 6~8-inch (15~20-cm) long pieces.
2. Wash the clam meat and oysters to remove sand by shaking in lightly salted water. Drain in a colander.
3. Cut the oyster into quarters.
4. If squid is whole, lay it on a cutting board. Pull the body and the tentacles apart. Cut the tentacles off just in front of the eyes. Discard the eyes, viscera, ink sac and backbone (small cartilage piece). Remove the skin from the meat. Wash the cavity of the body well to remove any sand. Cut the body open and lay it out flat, inside up. Once whole squid is prepared, or using pre-prepared squid, slice the body thinly into 1-inch (3-cm) long pieces and cut the tentacles into 1-inch (3-cm) long pieces.
5. In a bowl, combine the flour, water and an egg. Whisk them till a batter forms, and there is no lumps. Add pinch of salt to taste.
6. In a small bowl, beat two eggs well.
7. In another small bowl, combine all the ingredients of *cho-ganjang* and mix well.

Cooking

1. In a large cast-iron or nonstick skillet, heat 2 or 3 tablespoons of oil over medium-high heat. Dip the ¼ of green onions and Korean chives into the batter. Lift them out of batter and spread the vegetables on a skillet side by side into square shape. Spread the ¼ of clams, oysters and squid on top of the pancake.
2. Cover with a lid until the batter is cooked half way. Remove the cover and pour the ¼ of beaten eggs on top. When the bottom turns to brown, turn the pancake over carefully with a grill spatula. Pan-fry both sides until it is crispy and golden brown.
3. Repeat above methods and make 3 more pancakes.
4. Cut them into bite-sized pieces and serve with *cho-ganjang*.

Stir-fried Sweet Potato Noodles and Vegetables
Japchae 잡채

> This dish is made by mixing boiled sweet potato noodles, stir-fried vegetables, mushrooms and meat in soy sauce. Its characteristic is that each type of mushroom and vegetable is cooked separately before they are all mixed.
> Because of its colorful but classy appearance, *japchae* is one of the signature dishes of family gatherings. *Jap* means 'to mix, to gather,' and *chae* means 'vegetables.' In short, *japchae* is made by mixing various vegetables, and only recently have sweet potato noodles added to the dish.

Serves 4

7 oz (200g) beef (top round)
½ English cucumber (2½ oz, 75g)
Brine for cucumber
1 teaspoon salt, ½ cup water
½ onion (3½ oz, 100g)
⅓ carrot (2 oz, 60g)
3 *pyogo* (shiitake) mushrooms (½ oz, 15g after soaking 1½ oz, 45g)
3½ oz (100g) sweet potato noodles
1 egg
vegetable oil, salt as needed
Marinade for beef
2 tablespoons soy sauce,
1 tablespoon sugar,
4 teaspoons minced green onion,
2 teaspoons minced garlic,
2 teaspoons toasted sesame seeds, crushed, 1 teaspoon sesame oil, pinch of ground black pepper
Seasoning for noodles
1 tablespoon soy sauce,
½ tablespoon sugar,
1 tablespoon sesame oil

Preparation

1 In a small bowl, mix all the ingredients of marinade for beef. Cut the beef into julienne strips, along the grain. Marinate the beef for 20 minutes.
2 Cut the cucumber into 1½-inch (4-cm) long pieces, then cut it in half lengthwise. Remove the seeds. Cut the cucumber into ⅒-inch (0.2-cm) thick strips and marinade in brine for 10 minutes. Squeeze out the excess moisture.
3 Cut the onion into julienne strips.
4 Remove the stems of *pyogo* mushrooms and cut them into fine julienne strips.
5 Cut the carrot into 1½-inch (4-cm) long pieces, then cut into ½×⅒ -inch (1×0.2-cm) strips.
6 Soak the sweet potato noodles in lukewarm water for 20 minutes.
7 Separate egg yolk and egg white into two bowls and beat them well with a pinch of salt (How to make *jidan* garnishes 47p).

Cooking

1 Pan-fry the yolks and whites separately on a lightly greased skillet over low heat into very thin sheets. Cut into 1½×½-inch (4×1-cm) strips.
2 Heat the oil in a skillet and stir-frying separately in order, the onion, *pyogo* mushrooms and carrot, with a pinch of salt over high heat.
3 Heat a little oil in a skillet and stir-fry the marinated beef strips quickly, stirring to prevent them from sticking together.
4 Pour 4 cups of water into a medium pot and bring to a boil. Add the soaked sweet potato noodles and cook for 5 minutes. Turn off the heat and drain the noodles in a colander. Heat the oil in a skillet and stir-fry cooked noodles with the soy dressing for 5 minutes.
5 In a large bowl, put all the cooked vegetables, beef, noodles and toss to combine. Place them in a serving plate and garnish with fried egg pieces.

Tip

Serve at room temperature, but not too cold.
When selecting the vegetables to use for *japchae*, consider the harmony of five colors: red, green, white, black and yellow. Use carrots or red peppers for red; cucumbers, spinach or squash for green; bellflower roots, bean sprouts or oyster mushrooms for white; *pyogo* mushrooms or black tree mushrooms for black; and julienned fried eggs 47p for yellow.

P2 » P5

P6

C3

C4

C5

Toasted Laver Rolls

Gimbap 김밥

> *Gimbap* is easily made by seasoning cooked white rice with salt and sesame oil, spreading it over lightly toasted laver, adding various vegetables and beef and rolling and cutting them into bite-sized pieces.
>
> Because *gimbap* is easy to eat anywhere, it is a convenient dish for a simple lunch or as a lunchbox menu for outings or travels. In Korea, it is a signature menu item that mothers put in lunchboxes on outing days.

Serves 4

4 cups cooked white rice (2 lb, 920g) 78p
1 teaspoon salt
2 tablespoons sesame oil
4 sheets toasted laver
7 oz (200g) ground beef
4 pickled radishes (3 oz, 90g)
⅔ English cucumber (3½ oz, 100g)
½ carrot (3½ oz, 100g)
3 eggs
vegetable oil, salt, sesame oil as needed

Marinade for beef
2 tablespoons soy sauce,
½ tablespoon sugar,
1 tablespoon minced green onion,
1 teaspoon minced garlic,
ground black pepper as needed

Brine for cucumber
⅔ tablespoon white vinegar,
⅔ tablespoon sugar,
⅔ tablespoon water,
pinch of salt

Preparation

1 Prepare the cooked white rice. To prevent the rice from becoming too sticky, use less water than usual. While the rice is hot, mix with salt and sesame oil. Cool slightly for handling.
2 Marinate the beef with soy sauce, sugar, green onion, garlic and ground pepper for 20 minutes. Once marinated, stir-fry till fully cooked.
3 Cut the pickled radish into the length of the laver, and as the thickness of a pencil.
4 Cut the cucumber to the same length as the laver, and then remove seeds. Cut into strips as thick as pencils. In a medium bowl, combine the ingredients for the cucumber brine and soak the cucumber for 30 minutes. Then pat dry to remove excess liquid.
5 Cut the carrot into fine julienne strips. In a skillet, heat the vegetable oil over medium-high heat and stir-fry them. Season with salt. Let them cool.
6 In a small bowl, beat the eggs well with a pinch of salt. In a nonstick pan, fry the eggs into thick sheets and cut them into the same size strips as the cucumber.

Cooking

1 Place a sheet of the toasted laver shiny-side down on a bamboo mat. Put a cup of seasoned rice in the center of the sheet. Spread the rice evenly over the bottom ¾ of the laver. Make sure not to have an overly thick layer of rice or *gimbap* will not roll properly.
2 Arrange the beef, a slice of: pickled radish, cucumber, carrot and egg at the center of the rice. Making sure to alien them across the sheet. Roll the bamboo mat forward towards the non-rice covered end. While you roll, press firmly to shape the roll, while still remaining gentle enough as to not damage the laver.
3 Grease the knife with sesame oil, then cut the rolls into ½-inch (1-cm) thick pieces.

Tip

It is important to cook rice properly without too much moisture. Rice may be seasoned only with salt or by sprinkling a mixture of vinegar sauce made from vinegar, sugar and salt.
Season each ingredients seperately, and cook if needed.
Depending on the ingredients used, you can create variations of *gimbap* with different flavors and looks.
Brush sesame oil onto the surface of the *gimbap* according to taste or sprinkle sesame seeds on the *gimbap* and serve it in bite-sized pieces.

P1

P2

P3 » P6

C1

C2

Stir-fried Rice Cakes with Gochu-jang Sauce
Tteok-bokki 떡볶이

> This signature Korean street food is made by boiling bite-sized rounded rice cakes or thin rice cakes in *gochu-jang* (red chili pepper paste) sauce with vegetables and fish cakes.
> Chewy rice cakes with their spicy and sweet sauce are appealing. Recently, franchised *tteok-bokki* restaurants have become popular.

Serves 4

1 lb (500g) ½-inch diameter cylinder shaped rice cake sticks
3 sheets fish cake (3 oz, 150g)
1½ cups water (12 oz, 360ml)
Gochu-jang sauce
3 tablespoons *gochu-jang* (red chili pepper paste),
½ tablespoon soy sauce,
2 tablespoons sugar,
1 tablespoon corn syrup

Preparation

1 Rinse the soft rice cake sticks and drain. If the rice cake is hard, blanch in boiling water until soft.
2 Cut the fish cakes into 1×2-inch (2.5×5-cm) strips. Place the fish cake strips in a sieve and pour the boiling water over them for degreasing.

Cooking

1 In a saucepan, add water, *gochu-jang*, soy sauce, sugar and corn syrup and mix them together.
2 Bring the sauce pan to a medium heat, and cook the rice cakes, stir occasionally with a wooden spoon.
3 Add fish cakes, and continue cooking until sauce thickens.

Tip

Boil the sauce in a pan, add rice cakes and fish cakes, simmer for ten more minutes at low heat. This will insure the sauce absorbes into all of the ingredients.

Use an anchovy and kelp or meat stock instead of water to make a more savory dish.

More *gochu-jang* or a spicy pepper can be added if a spicier flavor is preferred.

P2

C2

Deep-fried Chicken with Sweet and Spicy Sauce
Maekom-dak-gangjeong 매콤닭강정

> This dish is made by deep-frying chicken and mixing it with sweet spicy *gochu-jang* (red chili pepper paste) sauce.
> Franchised deep-fried chicken delivery and takeout restaurants are popular in Korea, with fried chicken and seasoned spicy chicken as their signature items. Seasoned spicy chicken is made by mixing crispy, deep-fried chicken with *gochu-jang* sauce or soy sauce. Serving fried chicken and beer together is called '*chimaek*,' which is one of the most well-known dishes of Korea's late-night meal culture.

Serves 4

1 lb (500g) boneless chicken thigh (7 pieces)
½ teaspoon salt
1 tablespoon rice wine
2 oz (60g) roasted peanuts
¼ cup (1 oz, 30g) all-purpose flour or prepackaged frying mix
vegetable oil as needed

Batter
2 cups (8 oz, 240g) all-purpose flour or prepackaged frying mix
1 egg
1½ cups (12 oz, 360ml) water

Sweet and spicy sauce
1 tablespoon *gochu-jang* (red chili pepper paste),
1 tablespoon soy sauce,
2 table-spoons ketchup,
2 tablespoons sugar,
2 tablespoons corn syrup,
⅓ cup water (2¾ oz, 80g)

Preparation

1 Cut chicken into 1×1-inch (3×3-cm) bite-sized pieces. In a bowl, add chicken pieces, salt and rice wine and mix thoroughly with your hands. Marinate for 30 minutes.
2 Chop the peanuts roughly.
3 In another bowl, mix ingredients for the batter. The batter will have a runny, crepe like consistency.

Cooking

1 Dredge the chicken lightly with flour or frying mix, dusting off excess. Dip the chicken in the batter and deep fry at 340°F (170°C). Once completely cooked, place the fried chicken on paper towels or drying rack to remove the excess oil.
2 In a wok or a large saucepan, add all ingredients of sweet and spicy *gochu-jang* sauce. Heat the pan over low heat, stirring to prevent burning. Add cooked fried chicken pieces into the sauce and toss gently to coat. Add chopped peanuts tossing one more time and then serve.

Tip

Chicken can be seasoned with salt and pepper. The taste is better when the the meat is well marinated.
It is better to have a thin consistency of batter, because a thick batter will dry out.
To keep the batter crisp, first deep-fry the chicken initially, and then deep-fry it a second time just before mixing it with the sauce.

Rice, Porridge and Noodles

Huin-bap (cooked white rice) is the representative staple food in Korea,
but a multi-grain rice including barely, beans, and red beans is also used. *Juk* (porridge) is made
by boiling whole grain or ground grain in water with a variety of sub-ingredients,
such as vegetables, meats, and seafoods. *Myeon* (noodles) are frequently eaten as part of a simple
lunch, served to guests on festival days as the staple food. Noodles are mainly categorized into
three basic types according to broth: *janchi-guksu* (noodles in anchovy broth),
mul-naegmyeon (buckwheat noodles in chilled broth),
goldong-myeon (noodles mixed with vegetables and beef).

Cooked White Rice · Cooked Five-grain Rice

Huin-bap 흰밥 Ogok-bap 오곡밥

> *Huin-bap* is cooked by boiling short-grain rice in water. Only short-grain rice is used, and no mixed grains are added. The staple food in Korea is cooked, white, short-grain rice. It is soft and easily digestible, and it pairs well with various side dishes.
>
> *Ogok-bap* (five-grain rice) is a type of multi-grain rice that is cooked by adding glutinous sorghum, black beans and red beans to glutinous rice. The name is derived from the five grains added to cooked rice. Eating nine seasoned vegetables and *ogok-bap* with neighbors on the 15th day of the first lunar month is one of many Korean customs observed by most families. Additionally, people hope to attract good fortune by eating '*bokssam* (the wrap of good fortune),' which is *ogok-bap* wrapped in roasted laver.

Serves 4

Cooked White Rice

2 cups (1 lb, 450g) short-grain rice
2½ cups water (625ml)

Serves 4

Cooked Five-grain Rice

cups short grain white rice (1 lb, 450g)
1 cup glutinous rice (7¼ oz, 220g)
¼ cup dried red beans
½ cup dried black beans
½ cup sorghums
¼ cup glutinous millets
2½ cups water (625ml, 1 cup red bean cooking liquid,
1½ cups water)
½ tablespoon salt

Tip

Ogok-bap does not require the use of those particular five grains, and different grains may be used from time to time. Due to the glutinous nature of the grains used in *ogok-bap*, less water should be used to cook the rice in *ogok-bap* than is used to cook white rice.

Ogok-bap can be cooked in the same way as white rice, by adding water to a pot, or it can be steamed in a steamer on a hemp cloth.

Usually, when non-rice grains are used, they should be soaked sufficiently before cooking. However, this step can be eliminated when a pressure cooker is used.

Preparation

Huin-bap (Cooked White Rice)

1 In a medium bowl, rinse the white rice several times until water runs clear. Otherwise, the grains will be sticky when cooked. After rinsing add enough water to cover and soak the rice for 30 minutes and then drain.

Cooking

1 In a medium pot, place the soaked rice and 2½ cups water and cover the pot with the lid. Bring the pot to a boil over high heat.
2 Once the pot boils, reduce the heat to medium and simmer until cooked thoroughly for 20 minutes. Reduce the heat to very low and let it settle for 5 minutes.
3 Remove the pot from the heat and gently stir the rice with a wooden spoon. Serve in a bowl.

Preparation

Ogok-bap (Cooked Five-grain Rice)

1 Wash the short grain rice and glutinous rice until water runs clear. Add enough water to cover and soak them for 30 minutes and then drain.
2 Wash red beans to remove any stones or rocks. Then in a medium saucepan, put the red beans and enough water to cover. Bring to a boil over high heat, then drain and discard the water. Pour 3 cups of water to the saucepan and bring back to a boil. Reduce the heat to medium-low and cook until red beans are tender. Drain and reserve the red bean cooking liquid.
3 Wash the black beans to remove any stones and soak them for 2 hours.
4 Wash the sorghums and soak them for 2 hours changing water several times. Wash the millets and drain.

Cooking

1 In a large saucepan, combine the short grain rice, glutinous rice, red beans, black beans, and sorghums and mix well.
2 In a medium bowl, pour 1 cup of red bean cooking liquid and 1½ cups of water. Season with salt.
3 Pour the liquid over the rice mixture in the saucepan. Cover the saucepan with a lid and bring to a boil over high heat.
4 Place the millets on the top of rice mixture and reduce the heat to medium-low. Simmer for 25 minutes.
5 When the rice is tender but firm, reduce the heat to very low and cook for 5 more minutes.
6 Remove the pot from the heat and gently stir the rice with a wooden spoon. Serve in a bowl.

H-P1

H-C2

O-P1 » P4

O-C5

Kimchi Fried Rice
Kimchi-bokkeum-bap 김치볶음밥

> *Kimchi-bokkeum-bap* is made by stir-frying cooked rice with finely chopped *kimchi*. It balances the greasy taste of fried rice with the spicy taste of *kimchi*.

Serves 4

4 cups cooked rice (2 lb, 920g) 78p
7 oz (200g) *baechu-kimchi* (napa cabbage kimchi)
5 oz (150g) ground pork
⅓ carrot (2 oz, 60g)
½ onion (3½ oz, 100g)
4 eggs
4 tablespoons vegetable oil
1 tablespoon soy sauce
salt, ground black pepper as needed

Preparation

1 Prepare cooked white rice.
2 Chop the *kimchi* into ⅓-inch (1-cm) pieces.
3 Rough chop the carrot and onion into small bite sized pieces.

Cooking

1 Heat a large skillet over high heat. Add the vegetable oil and stir-fry the onion until it turns translucent. Add the pork, carrot and *kimchi*.
2 When the pork is fully cooked, add the rice and continue stir-frying. Finally season to taste with soy sauce, salt and black pepper.
3 In a separate frying pan, fry the eggs sunny side up style. Place the *kimchi* fried rice in the individual bowls and top each bowl with a fried egg.

Tip

Finely chopped beef, pork, chicken or vegetables may be stir-fried together according to the diner's preference. For a better combination, fried eggs are placed on spicy *kimchi-bokkeum-bap*.

Pumpkin Porridge
Hobak-juk 호박죽

❝ *Hobak-juk* is a porridge made by boiling peeled, steamed and crushed sweet or aged pumpkin and adding glutinous rice powder. ❞

Serves 4

2 lb (1kg) *dan-hobak* (kabocha squash or acorn squash)
½ cup (2 oz, 60g) glutinous rice flour or 2 tablespoons corn starch
6 cups water
½ teaspoon salt
2 tablespoons sugar

Preparation

1 Cut the pumpkins into halves. Remove the seeds and put them face down onto a work surface. Peel the outer skin and slice into ½-inch (1-cm) thick pieces.
2 In a small bowl, add glutinous rice flour and 1 cup cold water. Stir well.

Cooking

1 In a pot, put the sliced pumpkin and pour the 5 cups of water. Bring to a boil over medium heat, with a lid on, for 20 minutes.
2 Once softened, roughly mash the pumpkin in the pot.
3 While boiling the pumpkin, add the glutinous rice flour and water mixture and stir well with a wooden spoon.
4 Keep stirring until well combined to prevent lump forming. Add salt and sugar according to your taste. Simmer for 10 more minutes until it begins to thicken. Serve immediately.

Tip

The use of *dan-hobak* (sweet pumpkin) instead of aged pumpkin results in a more beautiful color and a sweeter taste. Red beans, beans, corn and chestnuts may also be boiled together.
Pumpkin can be finely crushed using a hand mixer. To enjoy a pumpkin soup, adjust the concentration by adding liquid such as water or milk.
When cooking pumpkin porridge with dry processed glutinous rice powder, add at least twice the amount of water as when using wet rice powder.
If glutinous rice flour is unavailable, corn starch would work in its place, but quantity might need to be adjusted.

P1

P1

P1

P1

C2

C3

Red Bean Porridge
Patjuk 팥죽

> This porridge is made by boiling rice in filtered red bean soup. *Dongji* (the winter solstice), which falls around December 22 or 23, is the longest night and shortest day of the year. Previously, the solstice was called a 'small new year,' and it was believed that a person becomes a year older only after eating *dongji patjuk*. People sprinkled *patjuk* over their gates and crocks because according to tradition, the beans' red color fends off evil spirits and prevents misfortune. *Patjuk* is also known as a dish shared with newly moved-in neighbors.

Serves 4

½ cup short grain rice
(3½ oz, 110g)
2 cups red beans
20 cups cold water
1 cup (7½ oz, 220g) glutinous rice flour
½ teaspoon salt
¼ cup boiling water
salt, sugar to taste

Preparation

1. Wash the rice till water runs clear and then soak in additional water for over 2 hours. Drain well in a colander.
2. Wash the red beans and drain. In a large saucepan, put the red beans with 5 cups of cold water. Cover the pot and bring to a boil over high heat. When it boils, drain and discard the water. Add 7 cups of cold water to the saucepan and return to a boil. Then, reduce the heat to medium-low and cook until the red beans are tender.
3. Roughly mash the red beans with a wooden spoon while they are still hot. Force the red beans through a strainer or food mill, adding 8 cups of water over the red beans and discard the skins of red beans on the strainer.
4. Let it settle for 30 minutes. It divides into two parts. One is the top part of red bean lquid and water, and the other part is the bottom solids of the red beans.

Cooking

1. In another small bowl, mix the glutinous rice flour and ½ teaspoon salt. Add ¼ cup of hot water and knead well till a dough forms. Make the dough into small balls ½-inch (1-cm) in diameter. In a medium pot of boiling water, parboil the dough balls for 5 minutes. Then put the parboiled rice balls into cold water and drain.
2. In a large saucepan, put the soaked rice and pour the liquid from preparation. Bring to a boil over medium heat. Stir occasionally and cook until the rice is completely cooked.
3. Add the pureed red beans to the saucepan and simmer over medium heat, stirring and scraping the bottom occasionally. Add the parboiled sweet rice balls and simmer for 2 more minutes. Season with salt and sugar to taste.

Tip

Simmer *patjuk* on a low heat for a beautiful red color.
Bite-sized small balls made from glutinous rice powder can be added.
Patjuk is generally seasoned with salt but may instead be seasoned with sugar, according to the diner's preference.

Buckwheat Noodles in Chilled Broth
Mul-naengmyeon 물냉면

Mul-naengmyeon is a dish of buckwheat noodles served cold in a soup of *dongchimi* (radish water kimchi) 186p and/or beef broth 40p. Radishes, pears and boiled eggs can be placed on top and may be seasoned with mustard and vinegar according to taste. Because *naengmyeon* is a cold dish, it is most often enjoyed during the heat of summer. However, those who like *naengmyeon* enjoy it at any time of year, and some argue that eating ice-cold *naengmyeon* in a warm, heated room during the cold of winter is a seasonal delicacy.

Serves 4

10 oz (300g) buckwheat noodles (for cold noodle)
7 oz (200g) white radish
½ English cucumber (2½ oz, 75g)
¼ Korean pear (5 oz, 150g)
1 red chili pepper (½ oz, 15g)
2 eggs
prepared hot mustard 46p, sugar, white vinegar, salt as needed to taste

Beef broth
7 oz (200g) beef (brisket)
10 cups water, 1 stalk leek (1 oz, 30g), 3 cloves garlic (½ oz, 15g), 1 teaspoon black peppercorns

Brine for white radish
1 tablespoon salt,
4 tablespoons white vinegar,
4 tablespoons sugar

Naengmyeon broth
5 cups *dongchimi* liquid (radish water kimchi 186p), 5 cups beef broth, 2 tablespoons salt, 2 tablespoons sugar, 2 tablespoons white vinegar, prepared hot mustard as needed

Tip

Mul-naengmyeon with *dongchimi* soup requires well-fermented *dongchimi* pickled in advance. Clear soup is made by mixing meat broth (from beef brisket or shank) with *dongchimi* soup. Asian grocery stores sell *dongchimi* for easily made *naengmyeon*. Otherwise, frozen *naengmyeon* soup is available in stores.
Korean prepared hot mustard is a thicker type of mustard with a stronger horseradish taste. It can be replaced with a spicy yellow mustard.

Preparation

1. Soak the beef brisket in cold water for 20 minutes.
2. In a large pot, put 10 cups water, beef, leek, garlic and black peppercorns and bring to a boil. When the beef is fully cooked and still tender, remove it and let it cool. Cut it into thin slices.
3. Strain the beef broth in a colander with cheesecloth and let it cool. Skim off all the fat from surface of the broth.
4. Cut the radish in ⅛-inch (3-mm) thick half-moon shape slices. In a bowl, combine the salt, vinegar and sugar and mix well, and then place radishes into mixture for 30 minutes.
5. Halve the cucumber lengthwise and cut diagonally in ⅛-inch (3-mm) thick slices. Sprinkle salt and set aside for 30 minutes. Squeeze out the excess moisture.
6. Peel the Korean pear and cut in half, then slice thinly. Cut the red chili pepper diagonally.
7. Fill a small saucepan with sufficient water to cover the eggs. Simmer the eggs for 12 minutes to prepare hard-boiled eggs. While simmering, roll eggs to keep the yolk in the center. Transfer eggs to an ice-water bath to stop the cooking. Peel the eggs and cut in half lengthwise.

Cooking

1. To make the *naengmyeon* broth, combine the chilled beef broth with the *dongchimi* liquid at a one to one ratio in a large bowl. Adjust the taste with vinegar, salt, sugar and hot mustard.
2. When the sliced beef, radish, cucumber, pear, chili pepper and eggs as garnish and broth are prepared, cook noodles. In the stockpot, bring 4 quarts of fresh water to a boil and add the noodles. Bring to a boil and add 1 cup of cold water. Then bring back to a boil and cook for 3~4 minutes or according to the package directions. Drain and rinse under cold water several times. Coil the noodles with your hands into a bird's nest shape for individual portions and let them drain in a colander.
3. Place the noodles in individual serving bowls and garnish with the slices of beef, radish, cucumber, pear, red chili pepper and eggs on top. Pour the chilled *naengmyeon* broth slowly not to disturb the noodle shape. Serve with prepared hot mustard, sugar and vinegar on the side.

Spicy Buckwheat Noodles
Bibim-naengmyeon 비빔냉면

> Like *mul-naengmyeon*, *bibim-naengmyeon* uses buckwheat noodles. Rinse in cold water, drain, top with sliced raw skate salad or beef, radish, cucumber and boiled egg, and serve cold with sweetened *gochu-jang* (red chili pepper paste).

Serves 4

- 14 oz (400g) buckwheat noodles
- 3½ oz (100g) white radish
- ½ English cucumber (2½ oz, 75g)
- ½ Korean pear (10 oz, 300g)
- 2 eggs
- white vinegar, prepared mustard sauce 46p as needed

Boiled beef slices
- 7 oz (200g) beef (brisket), 12 cups water, 1 stalk leek (1 oz, 30g), 3 cloves garlic (½ oz, 15g), 1½ oz (45g) ginger, 1 teaspoon black peppercorns

Brine for white radish and cucumber
- ½ cup water, ½ cup white vinegar, ½ cup sugar, 1 tablespoon salt

Seasoning for naengmyeon
- ½ onion (3½ oz, 100g)
- ¼ apple (2 oz, 60g)
- 4 cloves garlic (⅔ oz, 20g)
- 1 stalk leek (1 oz, 30g),
- ½ cup honey, ½ cup white vinegar, 1 tablespoon prepared hot mustard, 2 tablespoons salt, 6 tablespoons *gochut-garu* (red chili pepper powder), 2 tablespoons *gochu-jang* (red chili pepper paste)

Preparation

1 To make the brine for the white radish and cucumber in a medium bowl, dissolve the sugar in the water and mix in the vinegar and salt. Cut the white radish into 2×½-inch (5×1-cm) thin strips. Halve cucumber lengthwise, and cut them diagonally in ⅛-inch (3-mm) thick slice. Soak them in the brine for 30 minutes. And squeeze out the excess water.
2 Peel the Korean pear and cut into the same size as the white radish.
3 Place beef brisket in the cold water to drain blood. Put beef and 12 cups water in the pot. Add leek, garlic, ginger and black peppercorns and bring to boil until the beef is tender. Remove the beef from the broth and slice it thinly.
4 Fill a small saucepan with sufficient water to cover the eggs. Simmer the eggs for 12 minutes to hard boiled consistency. While simmering, roll eggs to keep the yolk in the center. Transfer eggs to an ice-water bath to stop the cooking. Peel the eggs and cut in half lengthwise.
5 Blend the onion, apple, garlic and leek together in a grinder. Add the honey, white vinegar, prepared hot mustard, salt, *gochut-garu* and *gochu-jang* to the mixture. Continue blending till incorporated.

Cooking

1 In the stockpot, bring 4 quarts of fresh water to a boil and add the noodles. Bring to a boil and add 1 cup of cold water. Then bring back to a boil and cook for 3~4 minutes or according to the package directions. Drain and rub them with hands under cold water several times. Coil the noodles with your hands to form a bird's nest shape and let them drain in a colander.
2 Place the noodles in the bottom of a bowl and garnish with slices of beef, pear, cucumber, white radish and eggs. Pour the spicy dressing over them and serve with prepared hot mustard and vinegar on the side.

Tip

Traditionally, noodles for *naengmyeon* were only made from non-glutinous buckwheat powder; now, however, sweet potato starch is added to provide texture.

P1 » P4

P5

C1

C1

Noodles in Anchovy Broth
Janchi-guksu 잔치국수

> *Janchi-guksu* is a dish of boiled wheat noodles with garnish and anchovy soup. *Janchi-guksu* served with hot broth is called *on-myeon* or *guksu-jangguk*. Long, white noodles are ingredients that symbolize longevity and are traditionally the signature food item on special banquet days such as weddings or birthdays, especially 60th birthdays.

Serves 4

14 oz (400g) dried wheat noodles, thin
½ Korean young squash (4 oz, 120g)
⅙ carrot (1 oz, 30g)
2 eggs
vegetable oil, salt as needed
Anchovy broth
20 dried large or medium anchovies for broth, 10 cups water, 1 tablespoon rice wine, 2 tablespoons soy sauce for soup, 1 tablespoon salt

Preparation

1 Remove the head and viscera of dried anchovies and put clean anchovies into a large saucepan. Pour 10 cups water and bring to a boil. Reduce the heat to medium and boil for 20 minutes. Strain the broth in a colander with cheesecloth and remove anchovies. Season the broth to taste with rice wine, salt and soy sauce for soup.
2 Cut the Korean young squash into ⅛×⅛×2-inch (0.3×0.3×5-cm) julienne strips. Sprinkle with 1 teaspoon of salt and set aside for 30 minutes. Squeeze out the excess moisture. Heat the oil in a skillet and stir-fry the squash.
3 Cut the carrot into ⅛×⅛×2-inch (0.3×0.3×5-cm) julienne strips. Heat the oil in a skillet and stir-fry the carrot slightly with a pinch of salt.
4 Separate egg yolks and egg whites into two bowls and beat each well with a pinch of salt. Pan-fry the yolks and whites separately on a lightly greased skillet over low heat into very thin sheets. Cut into 2-inch (5-cm) long julienne (How to make *jidan* garnishes 47p).

Cooking

1 In the stockpot, bring 4 quarts of fresh water to a boil and add the noodles. Bring to a boil and add 1 cup of cold water. Then bring back to a boil and cook for 3-4 minutes or according to the package directions. Drain and rinse them under the cold water several times. Coil the noodles with your hands into to form a bird's nest shape and let them drain in a colander.
2 Place the noodles in the individual bowls and pour the hot broth over the noodles to warm up and return remaining broth to the saucepan. Garnish with slices of squash, carrot, and eggs on top of noodles and carefully pour over remaining hot broth back into bowls.

Tip

Beef or vegetable broth may be used instead of anchovy broth 40p. Traditionally, five colors were used to garnish *on-myeon*; now, however, due to the inconvenience of preparing each ingredient, the garnish is often reduced to three colors 47p.
Zucchini may be used instead of Korean young squash.
To prevent the noodles from swelling excessively, they are prepared just before serving.

P1

P1

P2 » P4

C1

C1

Noodles Mixed with Vegetables and Beef
Goldong-myeon 골동면

> *Goldong-myeon* or *bibim-guksu* is a dish of boiled and drained wheat noodles with a garnish of beef, egg, cucumber and Korean watercress mixed with *bibim* sauce. *Goldong* means a mixture of various ingredients. In the past, beef and various vegetables were mixed together in soy sauce, but eventually, it became more popular to use a sauce made with *gochu-jang*(red chili pepper paste).

Serves 4

14 oz (400g) dried wheat noodles, thin
3½ oz (100g) ground beef
2 dried *pyogo* (shiitake) mushrooms (¼ oz, 10g)
½ English cucumber (2½ oz, 75g)
1 egg
vegetable oil, salt as needed

Marinade for beef and *pyogo* mushrooms
1 tablespoon soy sauce,
½ tablespoon sugar,
2 teaspoons minced green onion,
1 teaspoon minced garlic,
1 teaspoon sesame oil,
1 teaspoon toasted sesame seeds, crushed,
pinch of ground black pepper

Soy sauce seasoning for noodles
3 tablespoons soy sauce,
2 tablespoons sugar,
2 tablespoons sesame oil,
1 tablespoon toasted sesame seeds, crushed

Preparation

1. Soak the dried *pyogo* mushrooms in cold water for an hour. Remove the stems and cut into 1/16-inch (0.15-cm) thin slices.
2. In a small bowl, combine the seasoning for beef and *pyogo* mushrooms and mix well. Add mushrooms and ground beef and mix them well. Heat a skillet and stir-fry them in a small amount of oil till meat is cooked.
3. Cut the cucumber in half lengthwise, and then slice diagonally into thin pieces. Sprinkle with 1 teaspoon salt and set aside for 10 minutes. Squeeze out the excess moisture and stir-fry lightly in a heated skillet with small amount of oil.
4. Separate egg yolks and egg whites into two bowls and beat them well with a pinch of salt (How to make *jidan* garnishes 47p). Pan-fry the yolks and whites separately on a lightly greased skillet over low heat into very thin sheets. Once cooked, cut into 2-inch (5-cm) long julienne.
5. In a small bowl, combine all the ingredients of soy sauce dressing for noodles and mix well.

Cooking

1. In the stockpot, bring 4 quarts of fresh water to a boil and add the noodles. Bring to a boil and add 1 cup of cold water. Then bring back to a boil and cook for 3-4 minutes or according to the package directions. Drain and rinse under cold water several times. Let them drain in a colander.
2. In a large bowl, place the noodles and ⅔ of prepared beef, mushrooms and cucumber. Reserve the rest of beef, mushroom and cucumber for the garnish. Add soy sauce dressing into the bowl and toss well.
3. Divide the noodles in individual bowls and garnish with the reserved beef, mushrooms, cucumber and egg strips.

Tip

Goldong-myeon should be made before serving. Leftovers cannot be saved.
There is no set recipe for the vegetables used in *goldong-myeon*. Fresh and seasonal vegetables are suitable. Chopped *kimchi* is often served with the vegetables.

P1

P1 » P3

P5

C1

C2

Noodles in Broth
Kal-guksu 칼국수

> The name '*kal-guksu*' comes from the shape of the knife-cut noodles made from thinly kneaded wheat dough. Generally, squash and potatoes are boiled together.
> *Kal-guksu* is a type of '*jemul-guksu*' in which the noodles are boiled in broth instead of being boiled separately in water. As a result, the broth becomes relatively thick.
> In the past, *kal-guksu* was enjoyed as an early summer delicacy.
> People from the southern regions of Korea tend to work up a sweat by eating hot *kal-guksu* in the summer, whereas people from the northern regions tend to enjoy eating ice-cold *naengmyeon* in the winter.

Serves 4

1 lb (500g) dried knife-cut noodles, vermicelli style (or 1 lb (600g) fresh knife-cut noodles, vermicelli style)
½ Korean young squash (3½ oz, 100g)
3 stalks green onion (1 oz, 30g)
1 tablespoon minced garlic

Chicken broth 95p

½ chicken, with bones (about 1 lb, 500g),
3 stalks leek (3 oz, 90g),
¼ oz (10g) fresh ginger,
10 cups water,
2 tablespoons salt,
pinch of ground black pepper

Spicy soy sauce

3 tablespoons soy sauce,
4 tablespoons water,
1 tablespoon *gochut-garu* (red chili pepper powder),
2 tablespoons minced green onion,
1 teaspoon minced garlic,
2 tablespoons minced green chili pepper

Preparation

1. Wash the chicken and put it in a medium saucepan with the leek and ginger. Pour 10 cups water and simmer with a lid on for 30 minutes over medium heat.
2. Turn off the heat and remove the chicken and reserve the broth. When the chicken is cool enough to handle, remove the meat off the bones and shred into small pieces. Remove the fat from the broth and strain. Season the broth lightly with a pinch of salt and black pepper.
3. In a small bowl, combine all the ingredients of the spicy soy sauce and mix well.
4. Cut the squash into ⅛-inch (0.3-cm) thick rounds and cut into julienne strips. Slice the green onions diagonally.

Cooking

1. In a large pot, pour the broth and bring it to a rolling boil. Add the noodles and cook for 5 minutes. Stir the noodles to prevent them from sticking together.
2. When the noodles begin to soften, reduce the heat and add the prepared chicken, squash, green onion and minced garlic. Cook for 5 more minutes until the noodles are fully cooked and tender.
3. Ladle soup into the individual bowls and serve with spicy soy sauce to add flavors, according to your preference.

Tip

Bread flour which has high-gluten content gives more elasticity and a chewy texture. For a nuttier flavor, mix in bean flour.

When making *kal-guksu*, shake off any excess flour from the noodles to prevent the broth from becoming too thick.

Generally, anchovy broth is used for the clear soup, but for a fresher flavor, boiled clam soup may be used. Instant chicken broth may be used instead. Although it may also be more convenient to use instant chicken broth, take into consideration that the resulting flavor will be different from that of traditional Korean *kal-guksu*.

Sliced Rice Cake Soup
Tteokguk 떡국

> This dish is made from thinly sliced bar rice cakes made from non-glutinous rice, boiled in meat broth and served with various garnishes.
> *Tteokguk* is the first meal in the morning of the Korean New Year, which falls on January 1 of the lunar calendar. This dish is meaningful because it is believed that by eating *tteokguk*, a person ages one more year.
> The reason for eating *tteokguk* on New Year's Day is related to the round shape of the rice cakes. The white color and long shape of rounded rice cakes signify 'purity' and 'longevity', which is why the dish is the first meal of the New Year.

Serves 4

1 lb (500g) sliced rice cake sticks, fresh or prepackaged
3½ oz (100g) beef (brisket)
6 cups water
2 eggs
3 stalks green onion (1 oz, 30g)
1 tablespoon minced garlic
1 tablespoon soy sauce for soup
salt, ground black pepper as needed

Preparation

1. Wash the sliced rice cakes in the cold water and drain.
2. Let stand the beef in the cold water for 30 minutes to drain blood. Slice the beef thinly across the grain.
3. Pour the 6 cups of water into a large saucepan and bring to a boil. When it boils, add beef slices and reduce the heat to low and simmer for 20 minutes. Skim off all the fat and any foam that rises to the surface.
4. Beat the 2 eggs well with a pinch of salt in a small bowl.
5. Slice the green onions diagonally.

Cooking

1. Reheat the broth with the beef and bring to a rolling boil. Season the broth to taste with additional minced garlic, soy sauce for soup and salt and add rice cakes. Continue cooking for 5 additional minutes.
2. When rice cakes have softened, add green onion and beaten eggs and stir lightly. Return broth to a boil, then season it to taste with additional salt.
3. Ladle the soup in the individual bowls. Sprinkle a pinch of black pepper to taste.

Tip

When the rice cake in *tteokguk* is left too long in the broth and becomes too soft, it loses its unique chewy texture. Thus, the rice cake should be prepared just before serving.

Generally, beef broth is used to boil *tteokguk*, but sometimes, chicken or seafood broth is used (40p. for broth making). Add dumplings to *tteokguk* to make '*tteok-mandu-guk*' (56p. for dumplings).

Soups and Stews

Guk (soups) is a basic side dish served with every meal in Korea and accompanies the cooked rice.
Soup is largely classified into three types: clear soup, thick soup, and beef bone soup.
To make soup, meats are commonly used as well as almost any ingredients, including seafoods,
vegetables, and seaweeds. *Jjigae* (stews) is a broth-based food with a stronger taste than soup.
The distinctive feature of the stew is a nearly egual amount of solid food and broth.
Korean stews include soybean paste stew, red chili pepper paste stew
and clear stew, depending on the types of seasoning.
Jeongol (hot pots) is prepared in a bowl with marinated meats and vegetables,
and is cooked by pouring the broth over a portable burner on the table.

Seaweed Soup
Miyeok-guk 미역국

> In Korea, women who have just given birth receive a month of postnatal care and eat *miyeok-guk*. Dried seaweed is soaked in water and rehydrated and then simmered in clear beef or seafood broth. Seaweed is rich in calcium, which is an essential substance for the formation of bones and teeth, and iodine, which is an essential substance for the formation of thyroid hormones. Seaweed assists in womb contraction and prevents bleeding. Moreover, as one of the essential dishes of a person's hundredth day, first birthday and subsequent birthdays, *miyeok-guk* is one of the 'friendliest' dishes and is handed down through the generations.

Serves 6

7 oz (200g) beef (brisket)
1 tablespoon soy sauce for soup
1 teaspoon minced garlic
1 oz (30g) dried seaweed
2 tablespoons sesame oil
8 cups water
soy sauce for soup, salt, ground black pepper as needed

Preparation

1 Slice the beef thinly. Marinate the beef with soy sauce for soup and minced garlic.
2 Soak the dried seaweed in enough water for about 20 minutes to rehydrate. Cut the seaweed into bite-sizes and squeeze out the excess water.

Cooking

1 In a large saucepan, heat the sesame oil over high heat. When the oil is very hot, add the marinated beef and stir-fry until the outsides are browned.
2 Add the seaweed into the saucepan and stir-fry. Pour the 8 cups of water and bring to a boil over high heat.
3 When it boils, reduce the heat to low and season the soup to taste with soy sauce for soup and salt if necessary. Cook for 20 more minutes and add ground black pepper.

Tip

Store the dried seaweed in a air-tight container.
Miyeok-guk should be seasoned with soy sauce for soup and salt for clear taste.

P1

P2

P2

C2

C3

Spinach Soybean Paste Soup
Sigeumchi-doenjang-guk 시금치된장국

> This soup dish is made by boiling *doenjang* (soybean paste) and spinach in a broth of beef, dried anchovies or clams. *Deonjang-guk* is one of the most popular soups in Korea and is made by dissolving *doenjang* in water and boiling seasonal vegetables in the resulting broth.

Serves 6

- 7 oz (200g) spinach
- 3 oz (90g) beef (brisket)
- 8 cups water
  or 8 cups anchovy broth 42p
- 4 tablespoons *doenjang* (soybean paste)
- ½ tablespoon *gochut-garu* (red chili pepper powder) (optional)
- 1 stalk green onion (¼ oz, 10g)
- 1 teaspoon minced garlic
- pinch of salt

Preparation

1 Trim the stems of the spinach and rinse thoroughly. Cut them in half by hands if necessary.
2 Slice the beef thinly across the grain.
3 Slice the green onions diagonally.

Cooking

1 In a large saucepan, pour the water and add the *doenjang* and *gochut-garu*. Bring to a boil. When it boils, add the beef and lower the heat to low. Simmer for 15 minutes.
2 Add the spinach and minced garlic. Boil over medium-high heat until the spinach is tender. Add the green onions and season the soup to taste with salt if necessary. Cook for 1 more minute.

Tip

Spinach is a representative green leafy vegetable that is available all year round, it is the most popular vegetable used in *deonjang-guk*. Spinach may be replaced by chard, napa cabbage or bean sprouts. Beef or dried anchovies are popular ingredients for the broth and clams and dried shrimp may be used to improve the taste (40p. for making broth).

For a nutty taste, when using traditional Korean *doenjang* with a high quantity of beans, dissolve it in cold water and boil it for a long time.

P1

C1

C2

Chilled Cucumber Soup
Oi-naengguk 오이냉국

❝ This fresh-tasting cold soup is made by adding julienned cucumber to a cold broth seasoned with vinegar and salt.
Cold soup is refreshing in the summer and the fresh taste of cucumber and the sour taste of vinegar stimulate the appetite. ❞

Serves 4

1 English cucumber (5 oz, 150g)

Seasoning for cucumber
1 tablespoon soy sauce for soup, 1 teaspoon minced green onion, 1 teaspoon *gochut-garu* (red chili pepper powder)

Chilled broth
6 cups ice cold water,
4 tablespoons white vinegar,
½ teaspoon sugar,
pinch of salt

Preparation

1. Wash the English cucumbers clean. Thinly slice the cucumber diagonally and then cut into julienne.

Cooking

1. In a medium bowl, place the English cucumber strips and add soy sauce for soup, minced green onion and *gochut-garu*. Toss well.
2. In a large bowl, combine water, vinegar, sugar, and salt to make the chilled soup. Mix well.
3. Add the English cucumber strips into the chilled soup and stir well. Ladle the soup into the individual bowls.

Tip

Lightly soaked seaweed, or steamed and thinly shredded eggplant may be used instead of cucumber.
Since this soup tastes better served cold, store the garnish and soup separately in the refrigerator and mix them just before serving.

Soybean Paste Stew

Doenjang-jjigae 된장찌개

> This dish is made by dissolving *doenjang* (soybean paste) in water and boiling ingredients such as *dubu* (tofu), potatoes and Korean young squash in beef or clam broth.
> *Deonjang-jjigae* is common on Korean tables, and it is known as the dish that best represents nostalgic home cooking. An old Korean proverb counsels one to 'taste the *doenjang* rather than the stone pot'. This affectionate Korean expression about soybeans means that appearances are often deceptive.

Serves 4

- 3½ oz (100g) beef (sirloin)
- 1 package medium firm *dubu* (tofu) (10 oz, 300g)
- 7 oz (200g) potato
- 3 mushrooms *pyogo* (shiitake or button) mushrooms (3 oz, 90g)
- 1 onion (7 oz, 200g)
- 4 green chili peppers (2 oz, 60g)
- 1 tablespoon minced green onion
- 1 teaspoon minced garlic
- 1 teaspoon *gochut-garu* (red chili pepper powder)

Doenjang (Soybean paste) broth
- 2½ cups water,
- 4 tablespoons *doenjang*

Preparation

1 Slice the beef thinly.
2 Cut the *dubu*, potato, mushrooms, onion and green chili peppers into ½-inch (1-cm) cubes.

Cooking

1 Pour water into a medium saucepan and dissolve *doenjang* well. Bring to a boil and simmer for 10 minutes.
2 Add the beef into the soup, and bring to a boil. Skim off any foam that rises to the surface.
3 Add the potato and onion. Simmer over low heat for 15 minutes.
4 Add the *dubu*, mushrooms, green chili peppers, green onion, garlic and *gochut-garu*. Cook a little bit more.

Tip

No matter which ingredients are used, *doenjang-jjigae* tastes authentic because it contains traditional Korean *doenjang*, which is made with fermented soybeans in a natural environment. Korean *doenjang*, which is rich in beans, tastes better when it is dissolved in cold water and boiled for a long time on low heat. If Japanese soybean paste which is rich in wheat is used, dissolve the soybean paste and boil it briefly after all of the ingredients have been cooked.

P1 » P2

C1

C4

Kimchi Stew
Kimchi-jjigae 김치찌개

> This spicy soup dish is cooked by boiling well-fermented *kimchi*, pork, clams, *dubu* (tofu) and spring onions. Like *deonjang-jjigae*, *kimchi-jjigae* is one of the most common dishes on the Korean table, and it is suitable for lunch or light meals.

Serves 6

1 lb (500g) *baechu-kimchi* (napa cabbage kimchi)
7 oz (200g) pork belly (or 14 oz, 400g, pork rib)
1 package medium firm *dubu* (tofu) (10 oz, 300g)
4½ stalks green onion (1½ oz, 45g)
4 tablespoons vegetable oil
4 cups water
2 tablespoons soy sauce for soup
1 tablespoon sugar
pinch of salt

Preparation

1 Prepare well-fermented *baechu-kimchi* 174p and cut them into 1½-inch (4-cm) pieces.
2 Slice the pork thinly across the grain and cut into 1½-inch (4-cm) pieces.
3 Cut the *dubu* into 1×1½×½-inch (3×4×1-cm) thick pieces.
4 Slice the green onions into 1-inch (3-cm) long.

Cooking

1 In a large saucepan, heat the vegetable oil over high heat, stir-fry the pork till the porks are browned. Add *kimchi* and continue stir-fry.
2 Add water into the saucepan and simmer for 20 minutes. When *kimchi* is tender, add the *dubu*, green onions, sugar and soy sauce for soup. Cook for 10 more minutes. Season to taste with additional salt if necessary.

Tip

The taste of *kimchi-jjigae* depends on the level of fermentation of the *kimchi* used. The dish tastes sweet when made with less-fermented *kimchi*, and it tastes sour when made with more-fermented *kimchi*. In Korea, *kimchi-jjigae* cooked with well-fermented *kimchi* is very popular.

P1
P2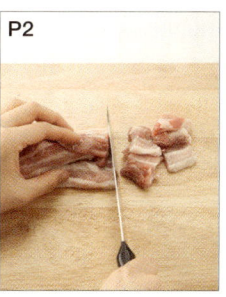
P3
C1
C2

Beef and Mushroom Hot Pot
So-gogi-beoseot-jeongol 소고기버섯전골

> "This dish is primarily made from beef and various mushrooms including oyster mushrooms, *pyogo* (shiitake) mushrooms and pine mushrooms boiled in a meat broth. In the cold of winter, families gather around the table and share a hot broth dish, the most representative of which is *so-gogi-beoseot-jeongol*."

Serves 4

7 oz (200g) beef (sirloin)
3 *pyogo* (shiitake) mushrooms (2 oz, 60g)
2 oz (60g) oyster mushrooms
2 oz (60g) king oyster mushrooms
5 oz (150g) mung bean sprouts
⅓ carrot (2 oz, 60g)
4½ stalks green onion (1½ oz, 45g)
½ onion (3½ oz, 100g)

Marinade for beef
2 tablespoons soy sauce for soup, 1 tablespoon sugar, 1 tablespoon minced green onion, 1 tablespoon minced garlic, 1 tablespoon sesame oil, pinch of ground black pepper

Broth
4 cups beef broth 40p or water,
1 tablespoon soy sauce for soup,
½ tablespoon salt

Preparation

1. Cut the beef into ¼-inch (0.6-cm) thin strips. Combine all the ingredients of the marinade for beef in a small bowl. Add the beef to the bowl and marinate for 30 minutes.
2. Wash the mushrooms. Remove the stems of *pyogo* mushrooms and cut them into thin slices and julinne them finely. Shred the oyster mushrooms into thin strips. Cut the king oyster mushrooms into 2-inch (5-cm) long strips.
3. Wash the mung bean sprouts and drain.
4. Cut the carrot into 2×½×1⁄10-inch (5×1×0.2-cm) strips.
5. Cut the green onion into 2-inch (5-cm) long. Slice the onion lengthwise.
6. Pour the broth or water into a medium saucepan, season lightly with soy sauce for soup and salt. Bring to a boil and keep hot.

Cooking

1. In a shallow hot pot, arrange the marinated beef and vegetables in clusters side by side in harmonious contrast colors and pour the hot soup over the arrangement. Heat the hot pot over medium-high heat.
2. When serving, heat the pot to keep the dish hot throughout the meal. Ladle into the individual bowls.

Tip

Being kept heated on a tabletop stove is a characteristic of *Jeongol*. Because broth is added occasionally while eating, it is best to prepare spare the broth in advance 40p.
Roots vegetables, such as carrots and radishes, are cut in advance and then parboiled in water before adding into the dish.

P1

P2 » P5

P6

C1

Spicy Beef Soup

Yukgaejang 육개장

> This dish is made by braising beef brisket, boiling vegetables (such as green onions) and seasoning the ingredients with *gochut-garu* (red chili pepper powder). In the past, Korean summer food developed to strengthen tired bodies in the summer heat. *Yukgaejang* is one of the signature health foods for coping with the heat of midsummer.

Serves 6

1 lb (500g) beef (brisket)
8 cups water
18 stalks green onion (6 oz, 180g)
6 cloves garlic (1 oz, 30g)

Spicy seasoning
3 tablespoons *gochut-garu* (red chili pepper powder),
3 tablespoons vegetable oil,
2 tablespoons minced green onion,
1 tablespoon minced garlic,
2 tablespoons soy sauce for soup,
2 tablespoons sesame oil,
¼ teaspoon ground black pepper

Preparation

1. Cut the beef into 4 pieces and soak them in cold water for 30 minutes to drain blood.
2. Pour the 8 cups of water into a pot and bring to a boil. Add beef, 3 green onions, and garlic cloves. Reduce the heat to medium heat and simmer for 30 minutes until the meat gets tender. Skim off fat and any foam from the broth.
3. Put the cooked beef into a bowl and shred them into thin strips or cut into thin slices. Let the broth cool and strain through cheesecloth.
4. Cut the 15 green onions into 2½-inch (6-cm) long. Blanch the green onions briefly in the boiling water.
5. In a small bowl, put the *gochut-garu*. Add the vegetable oil little by little and mix well to make the spicy seasoning. Add the minced green onion, minced garlic, soy sauce for soup, sesame oil and black pepper. Mix well.

Cooking

1. In a small bowl, mix the shredded beef with the spicy seasoning.
2. In a large saucepan, pour the broth and add the seasoned beef. Heat the saucepan over medium-high heat and bring to a boil. Add blanched green onions and cook for 5 more minutes. Season to taste with soy sauce for soup.

Tip

To make the broth, first of all, boil the beef brisket until cooked and saved liquid. Then shred meat along the grain. Add parboiled green onions to broth, with *gochut-garu* (red chilli pepper powder) *gochu-jang* (red chilli pepper paste).
You may also add mungbean sprouts, taro stems, and bracken.
Green onion may be replaced by leek.
When chicken (*dak*) is used instead of beef, this dish is called *dak-gaejang*. To make *dak-gaejang*, chicken is braised with green onions and garlic; after cooking, the meat is separated from the bones. Finish this spicy soup dish by braising the chicken meat with various vegetables in chicken broth seasoned with *gochut-garu*.

Gingseng Chicken Soup

Samgye-tang 삼계탕

> This dish is made by braising young, whole chicken filled with ginseng, jujube, chestnut, glutinous rice and garlic.
> As a healthy and balanced dish made with chicken and ginseng, this dish–along with *yukgaejang* (spicy beef soup) 112p –is the Korean dish that is representative of health in the summer.

Serves 4~8

4 whole chickens (cornish hens, 1 lb (500g) each, giblet removed)
20 cups water
1 oz (30g) green onion for serving
salt, ground black pepper to taste

Stuffing
1½ cups (11 oz, 330g) glutinous rice
4 fresh ginseng roots
8 cloves garlic (1⅓ oz, 40g)
8 chestnuts
8 dried jujubes

Preparation

1 Wash the cavity of the chickens under cold running water. Cut off the yellow tail fat and remove any excess fat inside the chicken cavity.
2 Wash the glutinous rice and soak in cold water for 30 minutes. Drain in a colander.
3 Peel the ginseng roots by scraping with a knife and wash under running water. Peel the garlic and wash.
4 Peel the chestnuts. Wash the jujubes.
5 Stuff the cavity of each chicken with the soaked rice, 1 ginseng root, 2 cloves garlic and 2 chestnuts. Twist the chicken legs and tie them with kitchen twine to keep the stuffing in.
6 Chop the green onions.

Cooking

1 In a large pot, place the 4 stuffed chickens and pour 20 cups of cold water. Cover with a lid and bring to a boil over high heat.
2 When it boils, reduce the heat to low and simmer for 40 minutes, skimming off any foams that rise on the surface.
3 Place each chicken into a large individual bowl or a small saucepan, and ladle the soup. Serve with the chopped green onions, salt and black pepper on the side.

Tip

It is simple to boil one portion of a small, young chicken in a stone pot. When larger chickens are used, half a chicken is one portion. When using chicken parts, boil boned chicken legs.
When fresh ginseng is unavailable, red ginseng or red ginseng extract may be used.
When eaten as a summer health dish, abalone may be added.

P1

P3 » P4

P5

P5

C2

Special Dishes

Gui (grilling) and *jeok* (skewing) can be made by grilling over the fire without
any special tools. *Bokkeum* (stir-frying) is prepared by cooking ingredients in
a dry skillet or with oil, stirring frequently until there is almost no water.
Jeon (pan-frying) is made by coating ingredients,
such as meats, seafoods, and vegetables, with the mixture of flour and eggs,
pan-frying in a skillet with enough oil. *Jjim* (braising or steaming) dishes are basically
categorized into two cooking methods according to the tenderness of main ingredients.
One is a braising method primarily for tough meats such as beef and pork rib. The other is
a steaming method primarily for soft and tender meats such as fish, shrimp, and shellfish.
Pyeonyuk (slices of boiled meat) is made by boiling a lump of beef or pork,
slicing into bite-sized pieces, and served with seasoning or salted shrimp.

Grilled Marinated Beef Slices
Neobiani 너비아니

> *Neobiani* is a dish made of sirloin or tenderloin, which are the most tender cuts of beef, prepared by marinating thick slices of meat and grilling them on a direct flame. Historically, *neobiani* evolved from '*maekjeok*,' which is an ancient meat dish. Due to the influence of Buddhism during the *Goryeo* Dynasty, primarily the prohibitions on shooting animals and slaughtering cows, along with abstention from meat, ancient meat recipes have long been forgotten. However, due to Mongolian influence, meat recipes were later recovered. During that time, a meat dish called '*seokhamyeok*' was created in *Gaeseong*, and the recipe for *neobiani* was established as a type of court cuisine.

Serves 4

1 lb (500g) beef (sirloin or tenderloin)
2 tablespoons pine nuts, ground

Marinade for beef
4 tablespoons soy sauce,
2 tablespoons sugar,
3 tablespoons minced green onion, ½ tablespoon minced garlic, 1 tablespoon toasted sesame seeds, crushed,
½ tablespoon sesame oil, pinch of ground black pepper

*optional for marinade
¼ Korean pear (5 oz, 150g, 5 tablespoons pear juice) or 5 tablespoons beef broth
2 tablespoons rice wine

Preparation

1. Slice the tender part of the beef, such as sirloin or tenderloin, into ¼-inch (0.6-cm) thick and score meat to make them tender.
2. Peel the Korean pear and grind it. In a big bowl, mix all the ingredients of the marinade for beef.
3. Pour the marinade over the beef and rub them thoroughly. Marinate the beef for 20 minutes.

Cooking

1. Prepare the charcoal grill over medium-high heat. Grill the beef both sides to the desired doneness.
2. Place them in a serving plate and sprinkle the ground pine nuts.

Tip

It tastes much better to grill on a direct flame over a charcoal fire rather than in a conventional pan. In grocery stores, thicker meat portions for steak, rather than thinly sliced meat, are readily available. These cuts are suitable for making *neobiani* 118p.

P1
P2
P2
P3
C2

Grilled Beef Short Ribs

Galbi-gui 갈비구이

> *Galbi-gui* is a favorite dish in Korea which is made by marinating thinly sliced beef *galbi* in soy sauce and then grilling it. Previously in Korea, because *galbi* was sold as a whole rack of ribs, it was not a common dish in ordinary homes except on special occasions or for family gatherings. However, in approximately 1939, a *pyeongyang-naengmyeon* restaurant in *Nagwon-dong*, Seoul, began to sell portions of the dish under the name *gari-gui*. The dish became popular and was named '*galbi*'. In the Korean language, *galbi* literally means 'rib' and can refer to either cooked or uncooked ribs. There are two perspectives on the origin of the name 'LA-*galbi*.' Some insist that the name came from 'L' and 'A' from 'lateral,' an English word meaning 'side'; others argue that the name originated from the direction in which ribs are cut across the bone in America. LA-*galbi* originated with Korean residents of Los Angeles who began to eat *galbi*.

Serves 4

2 lb (1kg) LA style beef short ribs with bones (½-inch (1-cm) thick and 8-inch (20-cm) long)

Marinade for beef
5 tablespoons soy sauce,
2 tablespoons sugar,
3 tablespoons minced green onion,
1 tablespoon minced garlic,
1 tablespoon toasted sesame seeds, crushed,
2 tablespoons sesame oil,
pinch of ground black pepper

*optional for marinade
¼ Korean pear (5 oz, 150g,
5 tablespoons pear juice) or
5 tablespoons beef broth
2 tablespoons rice wine

Preparation

1 Soak the ribs in cold water for 30 minutes to remove blood and drain. Remove any fat or silver skin.
2 Score both sides to make them tender.
3 Peel the Korean pear and grind it. In a big bowl, combine all the ingredients of the marinade for beef and mix well.
4 Pour the marinade over the ribs and rub them thoroughly. Marinate the meat for 30 minutes.

Cooking

1 Preheat the grill over medium-high heat. Grill the short ribs for 2~3 minutes on each side. Ribs could be grilled over charcoal, pan-fried or broiled in the oven.

Tip

Galbi (short ribs) meat tastes better when it is well marbled. *Galbi* can also be cut into 2½-inch (6-cm) pieces, separating the white fat and the tough skin, thinly slicing the meat to a ½-inch (0.5-cm) thickness and making fine cuts all over the meat.

Although it tastes much better to grill the meat over a direct flame, when using lean meat, it is wise to keep meat juicy by cooking it in the oven.

P1

P3

P4

Boiled Pork Wrapped with Napa Cabbage

Dwaeji-bossam 돼지보쌈

> This dish is served with thinly sliced boiled pork, radishes in a spicy sauce and pickled napa cabbage wrappers.
> Thinly sliced boiled meat is called '*pyeonyuk*', and pork *pyeonyuk* is also called '*jeyuk*'. In the 1980s, restaurants started to serve pork *pyeonyuk* with salted shrimp sauce and napa cabbage wrappers. This dish is where bossam originated from.

Serves 4

- 2 lb (1kg) pork lump (belly or shoulder)
- 5 cups (1.5L) water
- 2 tablespoons rice wine
- 4 tablespoons *doenjang* (soybean paste)
- 1 stalk leek (1 oz, 30g)
- 3 cloves garlic (½ oz, 15g)

Brine for napa cabbage
- 10 oz (300g) napa cabbage hearts
- 1 tablespoon salt
- 4 cups water

Brine for radish
- 1¼ white radish (1 lb, 500g)
- 1½ tablespoons salt

Seasoning for spicy radish salad
- 2½ tablespoons coarse *gochut-garu* (red chili pepper powder),
- 2½ tablespoons sugar,
- 2 tablespoons minced green onion, 1 tablespoon minced garlic, 1 tablespoon minced ginger

Salted shrimp sauce
- 3½ oz (100g) salted shrimp,
- 1 tablespoon white vinegar,
- 1 teaspoon gochut-garu (red chili pepper powder),
- ½ teaspoon toasted sesame seeds, crushed

Preparation

1 Cut off the root of the napa cabbage hearts and soak the leaves in brine (1 tablespoon salt, 4 cups water) for 30 minutes. When the cabbages become tender, rinse them under running water and drain.
2 Cut the white radish into julienne and sprinkle the salt and set aside for 30 minutes. Squeeze out the excess moisture.
3 In a small bowl, combine all ingredients of salted shrimp sauce and mix well.

Cooking

1 In a large sauce pan, put 5 cups of water and rice wine, and dissolve the *doenjang* in it. Add leek and garlic, and bring to a boil. Put the pork into boiling water and cook for 30 minutes until thoroughly cooked. Pork will be finished cooking if blood does not leave meat after being poked with chopstick or knife.
2 Slice the boiled pork into ¼-inch (0.6-cm) thick pieces.
3 Toss the salted white radish strips with *gochut-garu* to tint. Add the rest of the seasoning for spicy radish salad and toss well.
4 Place the pork slices in a large serving plate and arrange the salted napa cabbages and spicy radish salad on the side.
5 Serve with the salted shrimp sauce for dipping.

Tip

Belly and shoulder are the best cuts to make pork *pyeonyuk*.
Boiled meat slices can be dipped in salted shrimp and wrapped in napa cabbage *kimchi* or *bossam-kimchi*. Salted shrimp is a dipping sauce that also helps in digesting meat.
Add a small amount of green tea, black tea or coffee to the braising water can help mask the pork smell.

P1
P2
C1
C1
C3

Braised Chicken in Soy Sauce
Dak-jjim 닭찜

> *Dak-jjim* is made by boiling chicken in soy sauce. It originated from the traditional dish of *Andong* in the Korean province of *Gyeongsangbuk-do*.
> There is an old Korean proverb that says, 'The wife's parents catch a brood hen when the son-in-law visits.' The origin of this proverb is the traditional view that chicken helps to cure chills and to provide energy to weak bodies. *Andong jjimdak* has been enjoyed in traditional markets in *Andong* since the 1980s, and this cheap but generous cuisine, made from chopped chicken portions, vegetables and sweet potato noodles, is loved by people of all ages and genders.

Serves 4

1 whole chicken (or cornish hens, 2 lb, 1kg) cut into 2-inch (5-cm) pieces
1 white potato (5 oz, 150g)
½ carrot (3½ oz, 100g)
¾ onion (5 oz, 150g)
6 stalks green onion (2 oz, 60g)
3½ oz (100g) sweet potato noodles (8 oz, 250g, soaked)
1 oz (30g) fresh ginger
1 dried red chili pepper (½ oz, 15g)
4 tablespoons vegetable oil
3 cups water

Marinade for chicken
2 tablespoons rice wine
1 tablespoon salt
pinch of ground black pepper

Seasoning
6 tablespoons soy sauce,
3 tablespoons sugar,
2 tablespoons rice wine,
3 tablespoons minced green onion,
1 tablespoon minced garlic,
½ tablespoon toasted sesame seeds, crushed, 1 tablespoon sesame oil, pinch of ground black pepper

Preparation

1 Wash the chicken chunks with bones in cold water and pat dry. In a large bowl, marinate the chicken with rice wine, salt and black pepper for 20 minutes.
2 Cut the potatoes and carrot into 1×1×1-inch (3×3×3-cm) cubes. Cut the onion into eighths, similar in size to the potatoes.
3 Cut the green onions into 1-inch (3-cm) long pieces.
4 Soak the sweet potato noodles in lukewarm water for 20 minutes.
5 Peel and slice the ginger thinly. Cut the dried red chili pepper diagonally into ½-inch (1-cm) long pieces and remove the seeds.
6 In a small bowl, combine all the ingredients of seasoning sauce and mix well.

Cooking

1 Heat the oil in a skillet and add sliced ginger and dried red chili pepper. Fry them slowly over the low heat to make a spice-infused oil.
2 Add the marinated chicken into the skillet with the spice-infused oil and sauté over medium heat until the outsides are golden brown; you don't need to cook thoroughly. Set the chicken aside and drain the oil in a colander.
3 In a large saucepan, put the chicken with potatoes, carrots and onions. Add the seasoning sauce and mix well.
4 Pour the 3 cups of water, or enough to cover chicken pieces, into the saucepan. Bring to a boil over medium heat for 20 minutes. When the potatoes are cooked, add the green onions and sweet potato noodles and mix well. Reduce the heat to low and cook for additional 10 minutes.

Tip

Cook the hard vegetables such as potatoes and carrots from the beginning, whereas add soft vegetables such as spinach should be added and cooked briefly when the chicken is almost cooked.

P1

P2 » P5

C1

C2

C3

Spicy Braised Chicken

Dak-bokkeum-tang 닭볶음탕

> *Dak-bokkeum-tang* is also called spicy braised chicken or *dak-doritang*. It is made by placing cut chicken and potatoes into a pot and simmering it in a spicy sauce and water.
> This dish is intermediate between a soup, which has a large amount of broth, and a typical steamed or braised dish, which has a small amount of broth. It is relatively close to boiled-down cuisine.

Serves 4

1 whole chicken (or cornish hens, 2 lb, 1kg), cut into 2-inch (5-cm) pieces
1 white potato (5 oz, 150g)
½ carrot (3½ oz, 100g)
½ onion (3½ oz, 100g)
6 stalks green onion (2 oz, 60g)
2 red chili peppers (1 oz, 30g)
3 cups water

Marinade for chicken
2 tablespoons rice wine
1 tablespoon salt
pinch of ground black pepper

Spicy seasoning
4 tablespoons coarse *gochut-garu* (red chili pepper powder),
3 tablespoons *gochu-jang* (red chili pepper paste),
2 tablespoons soy sauce,
2 tablespoons rice wine,
1 tablespoon sugar,
2 tablespoons corn syrup,
2 tablespoons minced green onion, 1 tablespoon minced garlic, 1 teaspoon minced ginger, ½ tablespoon toasted sesame seeds, crushed,
1 tablespoon sesame oil,
pinch of ground black pepper

Preparation

1. Wash the chicken chunks with cold water to remove bone fragments and pat dry. In a large bowl, marinate the chicken with the rice wine, salt and black pepper for 20 minutes.
2. Cut the potatoes and carrot into 1-inch (3-cm) cubes. Cut the onion into eighths, similar in size to the potatoes.
3. Slice the green onions into 2-inch (5-cm) long pieces.
4. Slice the red chili peppers into ½-inch (1-cm) long pieces and remove the seeds.
5. In a small bowl, combine all the ingredients of spicy seasoning and mix well.

Cooking

1. In a large saucepan, put the chicken, potato, carrot and onion. Add spicy seasoning and mix well. Pour the 3 cups of water, or enough to cover the ingredients. Bring to a boil over high heat. When it boils, reduce the heat to medium and cook for 20 minutes.
2. When the liquid is reduced, add the sliced green onions and red chili peppers and mix well to season evenly. Cook for 5 more minutes.

Tip

To parboil the chicken, clean it in cold water and boil it in the sauce to remove the fat and odor.
Boil with hard vegetables, such as potatoes, and then add other vegetables, such as onions and spring onions, to preserve each ingredient's original flavor.

P1

P2 » P4

C1

C1

Grilled Mackerel
Godeungeo-gui 고등어구이

> "This dish is made by first sprinkling salt on halved mackerel and then grilling it on a gridiron or in a pan. Mackerel is one of the most common fish in Korea. Generally, fresh mackerel is used, but in inland areas where fish were rare, salted mackerel was traditionally used."

Serves 4

2 whole mackerels (1 lb, 500g, trimmed)
2 tablespoons salt
2 tablespoons vegetable oil

Preparation

1 Place the fresh mackerels on a cutting board and cut off the head, tail, and all of the fins. Cut open the belly and remove the intestines. Discard the head, tail, fins and intestines. Butterfly the fish. It is convenient to ask your local fish monger to butterfly the mackerel into fillets at the time of purchase.
2 Cut 3 or 4 slits into the fillets; cuts should touch the bone, and sprinkle coarse salt. Set aside in the refrigerator for 2 hours.

Cooking

1 Pat the marinated mackerels with a paper towel to remove the liquid that was released from mackerels.
2 Heat a broiler and a broiler pan. With a brush, lightly grease the pan. Lay the mackerels on the broiler pan with skin side-up and cook them until both sides are golden brown. You can also pan-fry the fish on the greased frying pan for convenience's sake.

Tip

In addition to mackerel, Spanish mackerel, sauries, hairtails, croakers or flatfish can be used for grilling.
For better taste, season the fish with salt before grilling.
For better taste, use a generous amount of oil in the frying pan or grill on a direct flame.

P2

P2

Spicy Stir-fried Squid
Ojingeo-bokkeum 오징어볶음

> This dish is made by stir-frying squids, onions, carrots and cabbage in a spicy sauce of *gochujang* (red chili pepper paste) and *gochut-garu* (red chili pepper powder).
> *Ojingeo-bokkeum* is easy to prepare as an appetizer because few ingredients are required and the procedure is simple.

Serves 4

2 whole squids (1 lb, 500g, trimmed)
⅓ carrot (2 oz, 60g)
¾ onion (5 oz, 150g)
2 green chili peppers (1 oz, 30g)
1 red chili pepper (½ oz, 15g)
6 stalks green onion (2 oz, 60g)
2 tablespoons vegetable oil

Spicy seasoning
2 tablespoons *gochu-jang* (red chili pepper paste),
1 tablespoon coarse *gochut-garu* (red chili pepper powder),
1 tablespoon soy sauce,
1 tablespoon sugar,
1 tablespoon corn syrup,
2 tablespoons minced green onion, 1 tablespoon minced garlic, 1 teaspoon minced ginger, 1 tablespoon rice wine, 1 tablespoon toasted sesame seeds, crushed, 1 tablespoon sesame oil, pinch of ground black pepper

Preparation

1 Lay the squid on a cutting board. Pull the body and the tentacles apart. Cut the tentacles off just in front of the eyes. Discard the eyes, intestines, ink sac, small beak and cartilage backbone. Cut the body tube open and remove the skin from the meat; hold the skin with paper towel and pull up to the head. (For greater convenience purchase prepared squids.) Rinse carefully under running water.
2 Lay the squid out flat–inside facing up–and score it diagonally with a knife about ¼-inch (0.6-cm) intervals: this will make it curl up when cooking. Cut the squid into 2×1-inch (5×3-cm) large rectangle pieces. It is convenient to use green onion knife. Cut the tentacles into 2-inch (5-cm) long.
3 Cut the carrot into 1½-inch (4-cm) long segments, and then slice into ½×1½-inch (1×4-cm) strips.
4 Cut the onion in half lengthwise and then cut them into julienne.
5 Cut the green chili peppers and red chili pepper in half lengthwise. Remove the seeds and slice diagonally.
6 Slice the green onions into 1½-inch (4-cm) long pieces.
7 In a small bowl, combine all the ingredients of the spicy seasoning and mix well.

Cooking

1 In a large bowl, mix the squids with the spicy seasoning. Add the prepared vegetables into the bowl and mix well.
2 Place a large skillet over high heat and stir-fry the seasoned squids and vegetables, until the squid pieces curl up and turn opaque, for about 5 minutes.

Tip

Squid becomes tough when it is overcooked. To make *ojingeo-bokkeum*, stir-fry the squid quickly on high heat.
Serve with cooked rice or thin (wheat flour) noodles.

P2

P7

C1

C2

Mung Bean Pancake

Nokdu-bindae-tteok 녹두빈대떡

> This dish is made by soaking, peeling and finely grating mung beans, adding minced beef or pork, mung bean sprouts and *baechu-kimchi* (napa cabbage *kimchi*), and frying them in an oiled pan.
>
> There is a popular song lyric that goes, 'Pan-fry a *bindae-tteok* (mung bean pancake) on a rainy day.' The origin of this lyric is the sound of pan-frying *bindae-tteok* on a generously oiled pan, which is similar to the sound of rain. This cuisine is most popular with *makgeolli* (unrefined rice wine), a signature, traditional Korean rice wine.

Makes 8 Sheets

- 1 lb (500g) dried yellow mung beans
- ½ cup water
- ½ lb (250g) ground pork
- 1 tablespoon soy sauce
- 1 tablespoon rice wine
- 5 oz (150g) mung bean sprout
- ½ lb (250g) well-fermented *baechu-kimchi* (napa cabbage kimchi)
- 1 teaspoon salt
- vegetable oil as needed

Garnish (optional)
- 1 oz (25g) green onions
- ½ red chili pepper (⅓ oz, 10g, or red chili pepper threads)

Cho-ganjang (Soy sauce with vinegar)
- 4 tablespoons soy sauce,
- 2 tablespoons vinegar,
- 1 tablespoon water,
- 1 tablespoon sugar,
- 1 teaspoon *gochut-garu* (red chili pepper powder) (optional)

Preparation

1. Soak the yellow mung beans in warm water for an hour. Drain and grind in a blender with ½ cup of water to make a thick batter.
2. Finely mince the ground pork and marinate with soy sauce and rice wine.
3. Blanch the bean sprouts in the boiling water and drain. Squeeze out excess water and chop coarsely.
4. Chop the *baechu-kimchi* into small pieces.
5. Slice the green onions and red chili pepper crosswise into thin rounds.
6. Combine all the ingredients of the *cho-ganjang* and mix well.

Cooking

1. Heat a skillet and stir-fry the pork. Set the pork aside to cool.
2. Combine the ground mung beans, mung bean sprouts, *kimchi* and pork. Season with salt.
3. In a large cast-iron or nonstick skillet, heat the vegetable oil to cover the surface over medium-high heat. Ladle about ½ cup of the batter into the hot skillet. Garnish with the green onions and red chili pepper on top. Cook till both sides are golden brown. Add more oil as needed. Remove the pancake.
4. Serve the warm pancakes in a serving plate with a small bowl of *cho-ganjang* for dipping.

Tip

Peeled dried mung beans are sold in Asian grocery stores.
This dish tastes better with finely chopped mung bean sprouts and bracken 166p.
For a smoother texture, mix soaked and grated short-grain rice.
After soaking, 1 pound (500 grams) of dried mung beans becomes approximately 2 pounds (1 kilogram).

P1

P1

P2 » P4

C3

Kimchi Pancake
Kimchi-jeon 김치전

> *Kimchi-jeon* is made by pan-frying flour batter with well-fermented *kimchi*. *Kimchi* is a very important Korean dish, to the extent that Koreans say that *kimchi* is all that is needed to empty a bowl of rice. There are many recipes for both *kimchi* and *kimchi-jeon*.

Makes 5 sheets

13¼ oz (400g) well-fermented *baechu-kimchi* (napa cabbage kimchi)
vegetable oil as needed
Batter
2 cups all-purpose flour
1½ cups water
1 egg
Cho-ganjang (Soy sauce with vinegar)
2 tablespoons soy sauce,
1 tablespoon white vinegar,
½ tablespoon sugar,
1 tablespoon water

Preparation

1 In a large bowl, combine the flour, water, an egg and whisk them until all lumps are gone.
2 Chop the well-fermented *baechu-kimchi* into ⅓-inch (1-cm) squares.
3 In a small bowl, combine all ingredients of *cho-ganjang* and mix well.

Cooking

1 Add chopped *kimchi* into the flour batter and mix well.
2 In a large cast-iron or nonstick skillet, heat 2 or 3 tablespoons of oil over medium-high heat. Ladle the ⅕ of mixed batter into the hot skillet. Shape into thin circle and pan-fry both sides until golden brown.
3 Make 5 pancakes and serve with *cho-ganjang*.

Tip

Kimchi-jeon is enjoyed as not only a side dish but also an appetizer or a snack.
Finely chopped pork, squids or clam meat is occasionally added.
To make *kimchi* less spicy, rinse it in water before mixing it into the batter. And to make it spicier, add more *kimchi* liquid.

Pan-fried Shrimps · Pan-fried Mushrooms

Saeu-jeon 새우전
Beoseot-jeon 버섯전

> *Saeu-jeon* is made with shrimp and *beoseot-jeon* is made with any kinds of mushrooms. Shrimp and mushrooms are great match for any types of *jeon* thanks to these beautiful color and shape. Also, they have nice chewy texture.

Makes 5 sheets

Pan-fried Shrimps
12 fresh medium shrimps
(10 oz, 300g) (8¼ oz, 250g, trimmed)
2 egg
pinch of salt and ground white pepper
½ cup all-purpose flour
vegetable oil as needed

Cho-ganjang (Soy sauce with vinegar)
2 tablespoons soy sauce,
1 tablespoon white vinegar,
1 tablespoon water,
½ teaspoon pine nuts, ground (optional)

Serves 4

Pan-fried Mushrooms
4 king oyster mushrooms
(10 oz, 300g)
pinch of salt
2 eggs
½ cup all-purpose flour
vegetable oil as needed

Tip

Any kinds of vegetables including, sweet potato, yam, acorn squash are good for pan-fried dishes.

Preparation

Saeu-jeon (Pan-fried Shrimps)

1 Wash the shrimp. Remove the head and peel off the shell, leaving the tail section.
2 Devein the shrimps with a skewer. With a knife, make several shallow cuts on the shrimp belly to prevent from bending while cooking. Or you may butterfly the shrimps.
3 In a bowl, beat the eggs well.
4 In another small bowl, combine all ingredients of *cho-ganjang* for dipping sauce.

Cooking

1 Sprinkle the salt and ground white pepper to shrimp. Dredge the shrimp in flour lightly except tails.
2 Dip the shrimps into beaten eggs, holding tails. Pan-fry them in hot oiled pan until golden brown.
3 Serve with *cho-ganjang*.

Preparation

Beoseot-jeon (Pan-fried Mushrooms)

1 Slice the mushrooms into ¼-inch (0.6-cm) thick pieces.
2 Sprinkle salt on the mushrooms and set aside.
3 In a medium bowl, beat eggs well.

Cooking

1 In a skillet, heat the vegetable oil over medium high heat. Dredge the mushrooms in flour and dip into beaten eggs.
2 Pan-fry them until golden brown.
3 Serve with *cho-ganjang*.

S-P2

M-P1

P3

C1

C2

Gujeol-pan 구절판
Platter of Nine Delicacies

" The term *gujeol-pan* originally referred to a serving plate separated into nine partitions. This dish evolved from *milssam* (beef and vegetables wrapped in wheat crepes). Place eight types of vegetables and meat in the outer cells of a nine-partition plate, and place wheat crepes in the center. Wrap vegetables and meat in a wheat crepe and dip it in mustard sauce. This dish is an ideal appetizer because of its colorful appearance and fresh taste. "

Serves 4

4 oz (120g) beef (top round)
⅔ English cucumber
(3½ oz, 100g)

Brine for cucumber
1 cup water, 2 teaspoons salt
3½ oz (100g) mung bean sprouts
⅓ carrot (2 oz, 60g)
6 dried *pyogo* (shiitake) mushrooms (1 oz, 30g after soaking 3 oz, 90g),
3½ oz (100g) small shrimps, peeled, deveined
3 eggs
vegetable oil, sesame oil, salt, pine nuts as needed

Marinade for beef
2 tablespoons soy sauce,
½ tablespoon sugar,
1 teaspoon minced green onion, ½ teaspoon minced garlic, 2 teaspoons sesame oil, 2 teaspoons toasted sesame seeds, crushed, pinch of ground black pepper

Flour crepes
1 cup all-purpose flour,
½ teaspoon salt, 1¼ cups water, 1 tablespoon vegetable oil

Mustard sauce 46p
2 tablespoons mustard powder,
1 tablespoon water,
1 tablespoon white vinegar,
½ teaspoon salt,
½ tablespoon sugar

Cho-ganjang (Soy sauce with vinegar) 46p
2 tablespoons soy sauce,
1 tablespoon white vinegar,
1 tablespoon water,
½ tablespoon sugar

Preparation

1. Cut the beef into fine julienne strips along the grain. Combine the ingredients of the marinade in a small bowl and add the beef. Marinate the beef for 10 minutes.
2. Cut the cucumber into 1½-inch (4-cm) long pieces. Peel the cucumber into a single, continuous paper-thin sheet while rotating the cucumber; stop cutting once seeds are reached. Cut the sheet into fine julienne. In a small bowl, make the brine and soak the cucumber for 10 minutes. Drain and squeeze out the excess moisture.
3. Remove heads and tails of the mung bean sprouts.
4. Cut the carrot into 1½-inch (4-cm) long pieces, and then cut into fine julienne.
5. Remove the stems of *pyogo* mushrooms. Slice them thinly, and then cut into fine julienne.
6. To make the batter of crepes, combine the flour and salt in a medium bowl then whisk water in gradually. Pass the batter through a fine sieve to remove lumps and set aside.
7. To make the mustard sauce, mix the prepared mustard paste 46p with the vinegar, salt and sugar. You could use commercial mustard paste instead of powder, and mixture of vinegar, sugar and water as well.
8. In a small bowl, combine all the ingredients for *cho-ganjang* and mix well.
9. Separate egg yolks and egg whites into two bowls and beat them well with a pinch of salt (How to make *jidan* garnishes 47p).
10. Finely chop the pine nuts.

Cooking

1. Blanch the mung bean sprouts in boiling water for 1 minute and rinse in cold water directly. Squeeze out the excess water.
2. Cook the shrimps in boiling water until they turn pink and are cooked thoroughly. Drain and set aside to cool. Cut the shrimps in half.
3. Heat sesame oil in a pan. Quickly stir-fry the salted cucumbers.
4. In another pan, heat sesame oil. Quickly stir-fry separately in order, the mung bean sprouts, *pyogo* mushroom, carrot with a pinch of salt.
5. In another pan, heat the vegetable oil over high heat and stir-fry beef quickly.
6. Pan-fry the yolks and whites separately on a lightly greased skillet over low heat to form very thin sheets. Cut them into 1½-inch (4-cm) long fine juliennes.
7. Lightly coat a non-stick skillet with the vegetable oil. Drop the spoonful of batter onto the pan to make very thin crepes about a 3-inch (8-cm) diameter. Cook crepes until the edges are opaque. Turn them over and cook a little more. Let them cool on a tray.
8. Layer the crepes in the center compartment of serving dish, sprinkling the powdered pine nut between the layers to prevent the crepes from sticking together. In each of the eight side compartments place each cooked vegetable separately, placing the same colors facing each other.
9. Serve with a small bowl of mustard sauce or *cho-ganjang* on the side.
10. To eat, put a little of every ingredients on a crepe with the mustard sauce or *cho-ganjang*, and then roll it up.

P2

P1 » P5

P6

P6

P7

C6

C7

Tip

Thick crepes do not taste as good as thin ones. Watery wheat batter makes thinner crepes. Alternatively, soft taco shells may be used.

Gujeol-pan is a signature cuisine that features Korea's five cardinal colors: red, green, yellow, white and black. Even though there are not set recipes for the vegetables, avoid vegetables with strong flavors, and prepare the equal amount of ingredients for each color.

If a nine-partitioned plate is unavailable, a large plate may be used.

Milssam is made by rolling together various vegetables within a wheat crepe. This tasty cuisine is convenient to prepare because guests can roll their own.

To serve *gujeol-pan*, provide each person with an empty plate. First, place a wheat crepe on a plate and add a small amount of eight different types of 3~4 ingredients. Add either mustard sauce or *cho-ganjang* and roll the crepe from one side.

Mung Bean Jelly Mixed with Vegetables
Tangpyeong-chae 탕평채

> " This dish is made by tossing mung bean jelly (made from mung bean powder) with five colored ingredients, including stir-fried meat, vegetables, julienned fried egg and laver, in a *cho-ganjang* (soy sauce with vinegar).
> The name of *tangpyeong-chae* is derived from discussion of the *tang pyeong* agenda for cooperation between different factions during the reign of *Yeongjo in Joseon* Dynasty. "

Serves 4

1 mung bean jelly (1 lb, 500g)
3 oz (90g) beef (top round)
3 oz (90g) Korean watercress
5 oz (150g) mung bean sprouts
1 red chili pepper (½ oz, 15g)
1 egg
1 sheet dried laver
salt, vegetable oil as needed

Marinade for beef
1 tablespoon soy sauce,
2 teaspoons sugar,
1 teaspoon minced green onion,
½ teaspoon minced garlic,
½ teaspoon sesame oil,
½ teaspoon toasted sesame seeds, crushed,
pinch of ground black pepper

Cho-ganjang (Soy sauce with vinegar)
1 tablespoon soy sauce,
1 teaspoon sugar, 1 tablespoon vinegar, 1 tablespoon water

Preparation

1. Slice off the hardened top of the mung bean jelly and cut into ⅕ × ⅕ × 2⅓-inch (0.5×0.5×6-cm) sticks. Blanch them in boiling water with salt and drain.
2. Cut the beef into julienne along the grain. Combine all the ingredients of the marinade for beef in a small bowl and add the beef. Marinate the beef for 10 minutes.
3. Tear the leaves off from Korean watercress and blanch the stems in boiling water. Shock in cold water and drain. Cut them into 1½-inch (4-cm) long.
4. Remove the heads and tails from the mung bean sprouts. Blanch them in boiling salted water. Shock in cold water and drain.
5. Halve the red chili pepper lengthwise and remove the seeds. Julienne them finely.
6. Separate egg yolks and egg whites into two bowls and beat them well with a pinch of salt (How to make *jidan* garnishes 47p).
7. Toast the dried laver. Place it in a plastic bag and break it into small pieces.

Cooking

1. In a skillet, heat the vegetable oil over high heat and stir-fry beef quickly. Set aside to cool.
2. Pan-fry the yolks and whites separately on a lightly greased skillet over low heat into very thin sheets. Cut them into 1½-inch (4-cm) long fine julienne.
3. In a big bowl, combine all the prepared ingredients, except some of stir-fried egg strips. Add *cho-ganjang* and toss them lightly.
4. Arrange them on a serving plate and garnish with remaining stir-fried egg pieces on top.

Tip

Muk or jellied food is made by boiling starch in water to make paste and then letting it cool. Starch can be made from mung beans, acorns, buckwheat or corn. Although *muk* does not have a particular taste, it has a distinct texture. For this reason, *muk* is generally served with vegetables or mixed with sauce.
Originally, this dish was mixed with *cho-ganjang* for a sour taste, but it can be freshly mixed with salt and sesame oil instead, according to the diner's preference.
Serve this dish as mixed or neatly prepared five-colored ingredients, place them around a plate and serve them with *cho-ganjang* to mix at the table.

P1

P1

P3

P3 ≫ P5 C1 ≫ C2

C3

Royal Stir-fried Rice Cakes
Gungjung-tteok-bokki 궁중떡볶이

> This court cuisine is made by cutting rounded rice cakes into bite-sized pieces, stir-frying them with beef, *pyogo* (shiitake) mushroom, onions and carrots, and seasoning them with soy sauce and sugar.
> Because *gungjung-tteok-bokki* is made without *gochu-jang* (red chili pepper paste), it is often called '*ganjang-tteok-bokki*' (soy sauce stir-fried rice cake). Adding beef and vegetables to the rice cake renders it nutritionally complete and gives a taste similar to that of *japchae* (stir-fried sweet potato noodles and vegetables) 68p. When replacing the sweet potato noodles with rice cakes, the dish is suitable as a meal.

Serves 4

1 lb (500g) 1-inch diameter cylinder shaped rice cake sticks
1 teaspoon soy sauce
1 teaspoon sesame oil
3½ oz (100g) ground beef
3½ oz (100g) mung bean sprouts
⅓ carrot (2 oz, 60g)
⅓ onion (2 oz, 60g)
3 stalks green onion (1 oz, 30g)
vegetable oil, salt as needed

Marinade
2 tablespoons soy sauce,
1 tablespoon sugar,
1 tablespoon minced green onion,
1 teaspoon minced garlic,
1 teaspoon sesame oil,
1 teaspoon toasted sesame seeds, crushed,
pinch of ground black pepper

Preparation

1 Cut the rice cakes into 2-inch (5-cm) long, and then cut each of them into 6 pieces lengthwise. Blanch the rice sticks in boiling water, if too hard. In a small bowl, combine the soy sauce and sesame oil. Put the rice sticks into the bowl and toss to coat them.
2 Remove the head and tail of mung bean sprouts. Blanch them in boiling salted water. until they turn to translucent. Rinse immediately in cold water and drain, squeeze out all of the excess water.
3 Cut the carrot into ½×1½×⅒-inch (1×4×0.2-cm) strips. Blanch them in boiling salted water.
4 Slice the onion thinly, and cut the green onions into 1½-inch (4-cm) long.
5 In a small bowl, mix all ingredients of marinade. Add the half amount of marinade to the beef in the bowl and mix well. Marinate for 30 minutes. Set aside remaining marinade.

Cooking

1 In a skillet, heat the vegetable oil over medium high heat. Stir-fry the beef for 3 minutes. Add the rice sticks and stir-fry.
2 Add mung bean sprouts, carrots and onions and cook together for 3 minutes. Adjust the taste with the remaining marinade and salt.

Tip

If the rice is larger or too long, cut into smaller bit size pieces.
To make it easier to cut, allow rice cake to dry slightly on counter.
Before stir-frying the rice cakes, parboil them in boiling water and mix them with oil and soy sauce.
This dish can be made by preparing the ingredients for *japchae* 68p and replacing the sweet potato noodles with rice cakes.

P1

P1

P2 » P4

P5

C1

Side Dishes

Jorim (braising) is a side dish made with strongly seasoned
and braised meat, shellfish or vegetables. White flesh fishes with a mild taste are
basically seasoned with soy sauce, and blue colored fish with
a rich flavor are generally seasoned with *gochu-jang* (red chili pepper paste) or
gochut-garu (red chili pepper powder), and then braised.
Namul (seasoned vegetables) are the most common side dish and
can be made with almost any type of vegetables.
They are originally consisted of a fresh salad and cooked vegetables.
A sufficient amount of sesame oil or toasted sesame seeds give a full-body flavor for
cooked vegetables. On the other hand, *cho-ganjang* (soy sauce with vinegar) or
cho-gochu-jang (red chili pepper paste with vinegar) is used as seasonal salad dressing.

Spicy Braised Fish
Saengseon-jorim 생선조림

> This dish is made by boiling fish and radishes in a pan with a spicy sauce. *Saengseon-jorim* is one of the most common grilled fish recipes in Korea.

Serves 4

- 2 whole hairtails (1 lb, 450g)
- 2 tablespoons salt
- ⅙ white radish (10 oz, 300g)
- 2 green chili peppers (1 oz, 30g)
- 1 red chili pepper (½ oz, 15g)
- 6 stalks green onion (2 oz, 60g)
- 1½ cups water

Seasoning for braising
- 2 tablespoons soy sauce,
- 1 tablespoon *gochu-jang* (red chili pepper paste),
- 1 tablespoons coarse *gochut-garu* (red chili pepper powder),
- 2 tablespoons rice wine,
- 1 tablespoon sugar,
- 1 tablespoon sesame oil,
- 2 tablespoons minced green onion,
- 1 tablespoon minced garlic,
- 1 teaspoon minced ginger,
- ½ tablespoon toasted sesame seed

Preparation

1. If the fish has not been prepared and cleaned by fish monger, snip the fins off with scissors. Then slice belly of fish to remove intestines, and wash the fish cavity. Cut into 2½-inch (7-cm) long pieces and sprinkle coarse sea salt. (It is convenient to prepare the trimmed cutlass fish for braising).
2. Cut the white radish into square pieces approximately 1×1×¼-inch (3×3×0.7-cm) thick.
3. Cut the green chili peppers and red chili pepper in half lengthwise and remove the seeds. Slice the peppers diagonally.
4. Cut the green onions into 1-inch (3-cm) long pieces.
5. In a small bowl, combine all the ingredients of marinade and mix well.

Cooking

1. In a medium saucepan, layer the radish pieces at the bottom and add half of the marinade for fish.
2. Pat dry the fish with a paper towel and place in the saucepan over the radish of **1**. Add the remaining marinade.
3. Pour 1½ cups of water to the edge and bring to a boil.
4. When it boils, reduce the heat to low and add the chili peppers. Simmer for 20 minutes without a lid, baste fish with the marinade.

Tip

For a less spicy dish, the fish can be boiled down in a sauce of soy sauce and sugar (*saengseon-ganjang-jorim* 150p).

You may use potatoes or carrots in case the radishes, a minor ingredient, are unavailable.

Spread vegetables such as radishes on the bottom of the pan to prevent the fish from scorching.

P1

P1

P2 » P4

C1

C2 » C3

Glazed Fish in Soy Sauce
Saengseon-ganjang-jorim 생선간장조림

❝ This dish is braised fish and radishes in a sweet soy sauce. ❞

Serves 4

1 Spanish mackerel (mackerel or salmon) (1 lb, 500g, trimmed)
2 stalks green onion (2 oz, 60g, white part only)
4 cloves garlic (⅔ oz, 20g)
½ oz (15g) ginger
vegetable oil as needed

Seasoning for braising
3 tablespoons soy sauce,
2 tablespoons sugar,
2 tablespoons rice wine,
2 tablespoons corn syrup,
pinch of tablespoon sesame oil,
pinch of ground black pepper,
¼ cup water

Preparation

1 If the fish has not been prepared and cleaned by fish monger, snip the fins off with scissors. Then slice the belly to remove intestines, and wash the cavity. Pat dry the fish with paper towels and cut it into 2-inch (5-cm) long pieces.
2 Cut the white part of green onion into 2-inch (5-cm) long.
3 Slice the ginger and garlic.
4 In a small bowl, combine all the ingredients of seasoning and mix well.

Cooking

1 Heat the vegetable oil in a large skillet over the medium-high heat. Place the fish pieces in it and broil them half, and then set aside in a plate.
2 Put the seasoning, green onion, garlic, and ginger in a skillet, and then bring to a boil. When the sauce boils, put the fish pieces in. Reduce the sauce until it thickens into a dark glaze, by pouring the sauce onto the fish.
3 Transfer the fish to a serving plate and pour the sauce over the top.

Tip

Use *kkwari* (shishito) peppers to mask the smell of fish with a subtle spicy flavor.
Use rich-flavored fish such as mackerel, mackerel pike, sardines or herring when using a spicy sauce; use sole, cod, red snapper or other delicate, sweet white fish when using a sweet soy sauce.

P1

P2 » P3

C2

C2

Braised Dubu in Soy Sauce
Dubu-jorim 두부조림

> *Dubu-jorim* is a side dish made by lightly frying *dubu* (tofu) in an oiled pan and braising it in soy sauce, *gochut-garu* (red chili pepper powder), sugar, green onions and garlic.
> *Dubu*, which is made from beans, is one of the most important sources of protein in vegetarian meals. In Korea, *dubu* is widely used in various dishes, including main dishes, side dishes, soup and *jjigae*.

Serves 4

1 package firm *dubu* (tofu) (10 oz, 300g)
½ tablespoon salt
1 tablespoon vegetable oil
1 tablespoon sesame oil
½ cup water

Seasoning for braising

3 tablespoons soy sauce,
1 teaspoon coarse *gochut-garu* (red chili pepper powder),
1 tablespoon sugar,
1 tablespoon minced green onion,
1 teaspoon minced garlic,
1 tablespoon toasted sesame seeds, crushed

Preparation

1 Cut the *dubu* into rectangles approximately 1×1.5×0.2-inch (3×4×0.5-cm) thick. Sprinkle salt and set aside for 5 minutes.
2 In a small bowl, combine all the ingredients of sauce for braising and mix well.

Cooking

1 Pat dry the *dubu* with a paper towel to remove exess water.
2 Heat the vegetable oil and sesame oil in a large skillet over medium-high heat. Carefully add the *dubu* pieces and sear until both sides are golden brown.
3 In a small saucepan, layer the seared *dubu* pieces, adding the sauce for braising.
4 When it boils, reduce the heat to low. While the *dubu* is simmering, continue to ladle the cooking sauce over the *dubu*. *Dubu* will be done once most of the sauce is absorbed.

Tip

Select firm *dubu* and lightly fry it in an oiled pan before boiling it in sauce to maintain its shape without crushing it.

P2

C1

C2

C3

Dubu with Stir-fried Kimchi
Dubu-kimchi 두부김치

> This dish is made by pan-frying well-fermented *kimchi* with thin slices of pork and serving it with warm, parboiled *dubu* (tofu). *Dubu-kimchi* is also popular as a relish with its combination of the smooth taste of *dubu* and the crispy texture of *kimchi*.

Serves 4

½ lb (250g) well-fermented *baechu-kimchi* (napa cabbage kimchi)
5 oz (150g) pork (belly or shoulder)
½ onion (3½ oz, 100g)
1 package medium firm *dubu* (tofu) (10 oz, 300g)
2 tablespoons vegetable oil
½ cup water
1 tablespoon sesame oil
pinch of salt

Spicy marinade for pork
½ tablespoon coarse *gochut-garu* (red chili pepper powder),
½ tablespoon *gochu-jang* (red chili pepper paste),
1 tablespoon soy sauce,
2 tablespoons sugar,
1 tablespoon minced green onion,
½ teaspoon minced garlic,
1 tablespoon sesame oil,
1 tablespoon toasted sesame seeds, crushed

Garnish (optional)
pinch of toasted sesame seeds

Preparation

1 Prepare well-fermented *baechu-kimchi* 174p and cut them into 1-inch (2.5-cm) long pieces.
2 Slice the pork into 1⁄10-inch (0.3-cm) thick and cut into bite sizes.
3 Cut the onion lengthwise into julienne.
4 Combine all the ingredients of spicy marinade for pork in a big bowl. Rub the marinade into the pork and set aside for 30 minutes.

Cooking

1 Cut the *dubu* into halves and place them in the saucepan. Add ½ cup of water and a pinch of salt and bring to a boil for 5 minutes. Remove the *dubu* from the water and cut into ½-inch (1-cm) thick. Place them on a serving plate.
2 Heat the vegetable oil in a skillet. Stir-fry the marinated pork.
3 When the pork is cooked half, add *kimchi* and onion. When the pork is cooked thoroughly, add sesame oil and toss well. Place them on the serving plate of **1**.

Tip

Dubu-kimchi goes well with *makgeolli*, a traditional Korean rice wine.
Vegetarians may omit the pork when pan-frying *kimchi*. In that case, spread a generous amount of vegetable oil in the pan.

P1 » P3

C1

C1

C3

Braised Potatoes in Soy Sauce
Gamja-jorim 감자조림

> *Gamja-jorim* is made by lightly stir-frying potato in an oiled-pan and boiling it down in soy sauce.

Serves 4

1 lb (500g) white potatoes
4 green chili peppers (2 oz, 60g)
2 tablespoons vegetable oil
Seasoning for braising
3 tablespoons soy sauce,
2 tablespoons sugar,
½ cup water,
1 tablespoon toasted sesame seeds,
1 tablespoon sesame oil

Preparation

1 Peel the potatoes and cut into 1-inch (2-cm) cubes and soak in water.
2 Cut the green chili peppers into ½-inch (1-cm) thick rounds and rinse in water to remove seeds.

Cooking

1 Drain the potatoes in a colander and pat dry with a paper towel.
2 Heat 2 tablespoons of vegetable oil in a skillet over medium-high heat. Add the potato pieces and stir-fry them for 5 minutes.
3 Add the soy sauce and sugar into the skillet and stir-fry. Add ½ cups of water, cover the lid, and simmer over medium heat for 10 minutes until the sauce is mostly absorbed.
4 When the potatoes are cooked thoroughly, add green chili peppers, toasted sesame seeds and sesame oil. Quickly stir-fry them together.

Tip

Sweet potato or sweet pumpkin may be used in place of potato. When the soy sauce has boiled down, evenly pour the starch syrup to finish for a glossy texture.

P1

C2

C3

C4

Stir-fried Dried Anchovy
Myeolchi-bokkeum 멸치볶음

> *Myeolchi-bokkeum* is made by stir-frying dried small anchovies without moisture. It comprises an important source of calcium in the Korean diet.

Serves 4

Stir-fried dried small anchovy
1 cup small dried anchovies (2 oz, 60g)
½ red chili pepper
½ green chili pepper
1 clove garlic (⅙ oz, 5g)
2 tablespoons vegetable oil
Mild seasoning
1 tablespoon soy sauce,
½ tablespoon corn syrup,
½ tablespoon sugar,
1 tablespoon water,
1 teaspoon toasted sesame seeds,
1 teaspoon sesame oil

Spicy stir-fried dried anchovy
1 cup medium dried anchovies (1½ oz, 40g)
2 tablespoons vegetable oil
Spicy seasoning
1 tablespoon *gochu-jang* (red chili pepper paste),
1 teaspoon *gochut-garu* (red chili pepper powder),
½ tablespoon minced garlic,
1 teaspoon sugar,
½ tablespoon corn syrup,
1 teaspoon rice wine,
2 tablespoons water,
1 tablespoon sesame oil,
½ tablespoon toasted sesame seeds

Preparation

Jan-myeolchi-bokkeum (Stir-fried dried small anchovy)

1 Put 1 cup of small dried anchovies into a preheat skillet over medium heat. Toast the anchovies without oil until crispy. Toss anchovies in a sieve or a fine strainer to remove powders.
2 Slice the garlic thinly. Cut the chili peppers into half lengthwise, remove seeds, and chop it roughly.

Maeun-myeolchi-bokkeum (Spicy stir-fried dried anchovy)

1 Remove the head and insides of medium-sized dried anchovies.
2 Preheat a skillet over medium heat then place 1 cup of medium-sized dried anchovies. Toast the anchovies without oil until crispy to remove fishy odor. Toss anchovies in a sieve or a fine strainer to remove powders.

Cooking

Jan-myeolchi-bokkeum (Stir-fried dried small anchovy)

1 Add the vegetable oil to a heated skillet and stir-fry small dried anchovies with garlic quickly. When garlic turns aromatic, add pre-stir-fried dried anchovies and stir-fry them together until they turn to golden brown and absorb the oil well. Set aside in a plate.
2 Put the soy sauce, corn syrup and water in the skillet and bring to a boil until it bubbles. Add the stir-fried anchovies back and stir-fry quickly. Add the chili peppers, sesame oil and sesame seeds and stir-fry a little bit more.

Maeun-myeolchi-bokkeum (Spicy stir-fried dried anchovy)

1 Add vegetable oil to a heated skillet and stir-fry medium dried anchovies over low heat. Set aside in a plate.
2 Add spicy seasoning to the skillet, mix well and bring to a boil. When it boils, add stir-fried anchovies back and stir-fry quickly over low heat. Add sesame oil and sesame seeds and mix well.

Tip

Add nuts or peppers when stir-frying the anchovies to reduce its salty taste.
For a neat and crispy finish, add sugar and reduce the amount of corn syrup. Conversely, for a moist finish, add additional corn syrup. To make *maeun-myeolchi-bokkeum* (spicy stir-fried dried anchovy), choose middle-sized anchovies. Good anchovies are well dried and not peeled, with naturally arched backs, and a silver-white color.

J-P1

M-P1

J-C1

J-C2

M-C2

Lettuce Salad with Cucumber
Sangchu-oi-saengchae 상추오이생채

❝ This salad is made by tearing the lettuce leaf off into bite-size pieces and briefly mixing them with *cho-ganjang* (soy sauce with vinegar).
This salad goes well with meat dishes; it can also be mixed with perilla leaves and onions. ❞

Serves 4

5 oz (150g) green leaf lettuce
½ English cucumber (5 oz, 150g)
1 oz (30g) chives
1½ oz (50g) chicory leaves
Cho-ganjang (Soy sauce with vinegar)
4 tablespoons soy sauce,
2 tablespoons white vinegar,
1 teaspoon *gochut-garu* (red chili pepper powder),
2 tablespoons sugar,
1 tablespoon toasted sesame seeds, crushed,
1 tablespoon sesame oil

Preparation

1 Wash the lettuce thoroughly under running water and drain. Tear them by hands into bite-size pieces.
2 Cut the English cucumber in half, and then slice thinly on a diagonal.
3 Wash the chives thoroughly under running water and drain. Cut into 2-inch (5-cm) long.
4 Wash the chicory thoroughly under running water and drain. Remove the stem of chicory, and then tear them by hands into 2-inch (5-cm) long pieces.
5 In a small bowl, combine all the ingredients of *cho-ganjang* and mix well.

Cooking

1 In a salad bowl, put the prepared leaf lettuce, chicory leaves, cucumber and chives.
2 Lightly toss well with *cho-ganjang* just before serving.

Tip

Cho-ganjang as a salad dressing is effective for weight control due to its low fat content and calories.
Meat dishes with lettuce wrappers or lettuce salad provide a more nutritionally balanced diet.
Other types of leafy vegetables may be used; it is convenient to use a pre-washed and/or pre-cut salad mix.
To enjoy the crunchy texture of the vegetables, toss with the *cho-ganjang* just before serving.

P1

P2

P2 » P4

C2

Fresh Kimchi
Baechu-geot-jeori 배추겉절이

> This is an on-the-spot *kimchi* made quickly by seasoning salted napa cabbage or fresh napa cabbage with *gochut-garu* (red chili pepper powder) and *aekjeot* (fish sauce). *Baechu-geot-jeori* is an on-the-spot *kimchi* that can be prepared quickly when fermented *kimchi* is unavailable or when one grows tired of sour *kimchi*.

Serves 6

1 lb (500g) napa cabbage hearts
4 tablespoons salt (2 oz, 60g)
3 stalks green onion (1 oz, 30g)

Seasoning
4 tablespoons *gochut-garu* (red chili pepper powder),
glutinous paste (4 tablespoons water,
½ tablespoon dried glutinous rice flour),
4 tablespoons water,
2 tablespoons anchovy sauce,
1 tablespoon sugar,
1 tablespoon minced garlic,
½ tablespoon ginger juice,
1 tablespoon toasted sesame seeds

Preparation

1 Trim off the stem of the cabbage. Tear the leaves into long strips, using hands or knife. Spread the salt evenly over the each leaf and set aside for 30 minutes. Rinse thoroughly in water and drain.
2 Wash the green onions and pat dry. Cut them into 1½-inch (4-cm) long.
3 In a small saucepan, to make the glutinous paste, combine water and sweet rice flour and bring to a boil, stirring constantly. When it boils, remove from heat and let it cool.
4 In a small bowl, combine the *gochut-garu* with the glutinous paste, anchovy sauce, and water to let the *gochut-garu* absorb the moisture. Add other ingredients for seasoning and mix well.

Cooking

1 In a bowl, combine the seasoned cabbage with the seasoning and toss well. Add the green onions and toss again.

Tip

When leafy vegetables such as lettuce are used instead of napa cabbage, season them with sauce just before serving to avoid wilting the leaves.
Add only a small amount of *jeotgal* to avoid a strong flavor, and prepare the sauce so that it is not too thick.

P1

C1

C1

Three-colored Seasoned Vegetables
Samsaek-namul 삼색나물

❝ This seasoned dish of parboiled or stir-fried vegetables may be served with three colors (white, brown and green) of vegetables on the same plate.

Food featuring seasonal vegetables reflects Korea's four distinct seasons. Above all, vegetable dishes are the essential condiments on Korean tables. In particular, three-colored vegetable dishes provide not only a color balance that is pleasing to the eye but also nutritional balance.

Samsaek-namul made of *kong-namul-muchim* (seasoned bean sprouts), *sigeumchi-namul* (seasoned spinach) and seasoned *pyogo* (shiitake) mushrooms. ❞

Serves 4

Seasoned bean sprouts
10 oz (300g) bean sprouts,
salt water (½ cup water,
1 teaspoon salt),
½ teaspoon *gochut-garu* (red chili pepper powder),
1 tablespoon minced green onion, ½ teaspoon minced garlic, ½ teaspoon sesame oil,
1 teaspoon salt, 1 teaspoon toasted sesame seeds, crushed

Seasoned spinach
10 oz (300g) spinach,
⅓ teaspoon salt (for blanching),
1 teaspoon soy sauce,
½ teaspoon sesame oil,
1 teaspoon toasted sesame seeds, crushed

Seasoned *pyogo* (shiitake) mushrooms
10 fresh *pyogo* (shiitake) mushrooms (10 oz, 300g) or buttom mushrooms, king oyster mushrooms, oyster mushrooms,
½ tablespoon vegetable oil,
¼ teaspoon salt, ½ tablespoon sesame oil

Tip

Almost all types of vegetables are suitable. Leafy vegetables such as spinach and chard are parboiled in salted water, and hard vegetables such as cucumber and radish are lightly preserved in salt and stir-fried. Dried vegetables are soaked in water before boiling and stir-frying. Mung bean sprouts and radishes are used as white vegetables; cucumber and chard are used as green vegetables; and various mushrooms and eggplants are used as richly colored brown vegetables.

Although bean sprouts are common in Korea, in other countries they are available only in Asian grocery stores. Mung bean sprouts may replace bean sprouts. The heads of bean sprouts are fully cooked by boiling for more than 10 minutes, whereas mung bean sprouts are fully cooked after only two minutes. When using bitter-tasting vegetables, parboil them in water to remove their bitterness before seasoning. Additionally, when using vegetables with rich flavors, do not use excessive seasoning such as green onions and garlic.

Preparation

Kong-namul-muchim (Seasoned bean sprouts)

Remove the tails of bean sprouts and rinse thoroughly. In a large saucepan, place the bean sprouts, salt and water. Put the lid on and boil for 15 minutes.

Sigeumchi-namul (Seasoned spinach)

Trim the stem of spinach and blanch in boiling water with salt for 1 minute. Rinse immediately in ice cold water and drain in a colander. Squeeze out all of the excess water from the spinach. If spinach is large, cut into 2-inch (5-cm) length, if too long.

Beoseot-namul (Seasoned *pyogo* mushrooms)

Remove the stems of fresh *pyogo* mushrooms. Rinse in the water and pat dry. Cut into julienne strips.

Cooking

Seasoned bean sprouts

In a large bowl, combine the *gochut-garu*, minced green onion, minced garlic, sesame oil, salt, and crushed sesame seeds. Add the cooked bean sprouts and toss well.

Seasoned spinach

In a large bowl, combine the sesame oil, salt, soy sauce, and crushed toasted sesame seeds. Add the cooked spinach and toss well.

Seasoned *pyogo* mushrooms

In a skillet, heat the vegetable oil over medium-high heat. Stir-fry the mushrooms with salt. Add the sesame oil at the last minute to flavor.

K-P1

S-P1

B-P1

B-P1

K-C1

Seasoned Bracken · Seasoned Bellflower Roots
Gosari-namul 고사리나물
Doraji-namul 도라지나물

> *Gosari-namul* has unique texture. *Doraji-namul* has to remove bitterness beforeing it. It is rich in fiber and chewy. These seasoned vegetables go well with *bibimbap* (rice mixed with vegetables and beef) 52p.

Serves 4

Seasoned bracken
1½ oz (45g) *gosari* (dried bracken) (10 oz, 300g, soaked)
1 tablespoon vegetable oil
4 tablespoons water

Seasoning
2 tablespoons soy sauce for soup,
1 tablespoon minced green onion, ½ tablespoon minced garlic,
½ tablespoon toasted sesame seeds, crushed,
1 tablespoon sesame oil,
pinch of ground black pepper,

Serves 4

Seasoned bellflower roots
8 oz (240g) *doraji* (bellflower roots),
1 teaspoon salt,
¼ cup water,
1 tablespoon vegetable oil,
3 tablespoons water,
½ tablespoon toasted sesame seeds, crushed,
½ tablespoon sesame oil

Seasoning
1 tablespoon sesame oil,
½ tablespoon salt,
1 tablespoon minced green onion,
½ teaspoon minced garlic,
½ tablespoon soy sauce for soup

Garnish (optional)
red chili pepper threads

Preparation

Gosari-namul (Seasond bracken)

1. Soak the dried bracken in cold water for 30 minutes and drain. In a pot, bring enough water to boil and put the soaked bracken, and then cook for 30 minutes.
2. Cut the cooked bracken into 2-inch (5-cm) length. In a bowl, combine all ingredients for seasoning. Toss well and marinade them for 20 minutes.

Cooking

1. In a skillet, heat the vegetable oil. Stir-fry marinated bracken and add 4 tablespoons of water. Cover the lid and cook until the water is gone.
2. Add the crushed sesame seeds, sesame oil, salt, and ground black pepper, and then stir-fry 1 more minute. Let them cool.

Preparation

Doraji-namul (Seasoned bellflower roots)

1. Wash the bellflower roots and cut them into 2-inch (5-cm) long strips. Put into a bowl, and add water and salt. Rub them well and wash to remove bitter taste. Blanch them in boiling water and shock in cold water. Drain and squeeze out the moisture.

Cooking

1. In a skillet, heat the vegetable oil. Stir-fry the bellflower roots over medium heat. Add seasonings and mix well. Add 3 tablespoons of water and cover the lid. Cook until the water is almost gone.
2. Add crushed sesame seeds and sesame oil. Toss well and let them cool.

G-P1

G-P1

G-P2

G-C1

D-P1

D-P1

D-P1

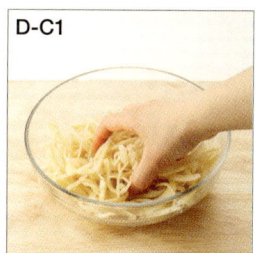
D-C1

Gyeran-jjim 계란찜

Steamed Eggs

"This dish is made by beating eggs with water, seasoning with salt and steaming them. This recipe's warm and smooth taste make it one of Korea's signature egg dishes, and it stimulates the appetite."

Serves 4

- 4 eggs
- 2 cups water
- 2 teaspoons salt
- 4 oz (120g) small shrimp meat
- 1 stalk green onion (¼ oz, 10g)

Preparation

1. In a small bowl, combine all of eggs, water and salt and whisk well until fully mixed. Strain them through a fine sieve and skim off any foam on the surface.
2. Chop the green onion. Wash the small shrimp meat in the salted water and drain.
3. Place a steamer holding 2-inch (5-cm) water over medium-high heat. Bring the water to a simmer for 10 minutes.

Cooking

1. Place the small shrimps into 4 small bowls.
2. Divide the beaten eggs among the bowls. Put the chopped green onion on top.
3. Set the eggs in the top of a steamer of **2** over medium-low heat, put the lid on, and steam for 15 minutes. To test for doneness, insert a toothpick. If it comes out clean, the steamed egg is done.

Tip

To make steamed egg smooth, beat eggs well without any foam on the surface and strain them through a fine sieve in order to remove the chalaza.

In addition to shrimp, various ingredients such as spring onions, mushrooms, carrots and chicken may be added to the egg mixture.

Steamed egg can be easily prepared using a microwave oven. Mix the egg and other ingredients together in a microwave-safe container, heat the mixture for three minutes and stir. Heat it for another three minutes, stir and then heat it for one more minute to finish. Heating time may be adjusted according to the power of the microwave oven.

P1

P1

P2

Rolled Omelet
Gyeran-mari 계란말이

❝ This dish is made by adding vegetables, such as chopped green onions, to beaten eggs, seasoning the mixture with salt, while pouring small portions of egg mixture into an oiled pan, and rolling it carefully over low heat.
This is one of the most popular lunchbox condiments. Numerous variations are possible. ❞

Serves 4

4 eggs
3 stalks green onion (1 oz, 30g)
½ tablespoon salt
vegetable oil as needed

Preparation

1 In a medium bowl, beat the eggs well with a pair of chopsticks.
2 Wash the green onions and finely chop them.

Cooking

1 Combine beaten eggs and chopped green onion in a bowl. Season with the salt and mix well.
2 Heat a rectangular skillet over medium-low heat and add the vegetable oil. Pour the egg mixture into the skillet. When the eggs are cooked half, lift one end of the egg about ¾-inch (2-cm), using a spatula or a pair of chopsticks, and fold it over to the other side. Repeat the process with the remaining egg mixture until you reach to the end of the pan.
3 Keep the heat low enough that the egg doesn't turn to brown, but rather stay soft and creamy.
4 Transfer the rolled omelet to a plate and let it cool. If you have a bamboo mat, shape the rolled omelet into a rectangle.
5 Cut the omelet into bite-size pieces and place them on a serving plate.

Tip

Add kelp broth and *cheongju* (refined rice wine) for a smoother and tastier *gyeran-mari*.
When rolling the egg, numerous variations are possible by varying minor ingredients such as laver or *kimchi*.

Kimchi

Kimchi is the most basic side dish that is made through
a process of brining and fermenting. It has an unique acidic taste caused by
the lactic acid producing organisms during fermentation and it not
only helps digestion, but also stimulates appetite.

Whole Cabbage Kimchi
Baechu-kimchi 배추김치

 Baechu-kimchi is made by stuffing julienned radishes, *gochut-garu* (red chili pepper powder), green onions, garlic and *jeotgal* (fish sauce) between whole cabbage leaves preserved in salt.
Kimchi is Korea's most famous food and is an essential food item on the table at almost every meal. Korea's *gimjang* culture, which refers to the culture in which a huge amount of *kimchi* is prepared for the cold winter, was designated a Masterpiece of the Oral and Intangible Heritage of Humanity by UNESCO in 2013.
Whole-cabbage *kimchi* is the most common type of *kimchi* in Korea and the most common item preserved during *gimjang*. There are different regional characteristics in the types of *jeotgal* (fish sauce) and seasonings used to make *kimchi*.

Yield 10 heads (10 gal, 40kg)

10 napa cabbages (about 44 lb, 20kg)

Brine for cabbage
4 lb (2kg) natural sea salt,
5 gal (20L) water

Filling
3 white radishes (12 lb, 6kg)
50 stalks green onion (1 lb, 500g)
10 stalks thick green onion (10 oz, 300g)
½ Korean pear (10 oz, 300g)
14 oz (400g) salted shrimp
3 cups (750ml) water
1¾~2 lb (0.8~1kg) coarse *gochut-garu* (red chili pepper powder)
1lb (500g) anchovy sauce (or fish sauce)
10 oz (300g) minced garlic
2½ oz (75g) minced ginger
2 tablespoons salt
½ cup sugar

Glutinous paste
½ cup wet glutinous rice flour
2 cups water

***Kimchi* liquid**
½ gal (2L) water
1 tablespoon natural sea salt
salt to taste

Preparation

Brining napa cabbages

1 Remove the tough or discolored outside leaves of the cabbages and trim off the stem. With a knife, cut the cabbages lengthwise into halves or quarters, depending on size of cabbage.
2 Dissolve half of the natural sea salt (2 lb) in 20 liter of water to make the brine, and soak the cabbage in the brine. Remove the cabbage from the brine and sprinkle the remaining natural sea salt (2 lb) evenly between the leaves. In a large container, put the cabbages neatly and pour the brine over. Let them stand for 6~8 hours making sure cabbage stays submerged, using stones. Rotate the cabbages from the bottom to the top.
3 Remove the cabbages from the brine if they are well bent. Rinse the cabbages thoroughly under running water several times and place them cut side down in a colander to drain.

Filling

4 Wash the white radishes clean and peel. Slice them crosswise into ⅛-inch (3-mm) thick rounds and then cut into julienne. It is convenient to use a slicer or a grater.
5 Wash the green onions and cut into 1½-inch (4-cm) long, and slice the thick green onion diagonally.
6 Cut the Korean pear into julienne.
7 Chop the salted shrimp roughly and preserve the liquid.
8 To make the glutinous paste, in a small saucepan, mix the glutinous rice flour and water. Bring to a boil and reduce the heat to low. Gently cook, stirring constantly with a whisk, until it becomes a paste without lumps. Let it cool.
9 In a large bowl, mix *gochut-garu* in 3 cups of water and let stand for 10 minutes. Add the glutinous paste, salted shrimp, anchovy sauce, and mix well to make *gochut-garu* paste.

P1

P3

P4 » P6

Cooking

Filling

1. In a large bowl, combine the white radish strips and *gochut-garu* paste and toss gently to tint the radish. Season with 2 tablespoons of salt and ½ cup of sugar.
2. Add the minced garlic, minced ginger, salted shrimp and mix well. Add the green onions, thick green onions, Korean pear strips and toss gently. Adjust the taste with salt or sugar, if necessary.

Stuffing

3. Working from the outside in, insert the filling between the leaves of the cabbages, making sure to coat every cabbage leave with filling.
4. Wrap tightly around the each stuffed cabbage with the largest outer leaf of the cabbage. Transfer into a container and place the cut side of the cabbage up. Pile them up neatly and press down firmly. Fill the container up to 80%.
5. Pour ½ gal (2L) of water into the bowl that cabbage was mixed and add 1 tablespoon of salt. Pour over the *kimchi*. All must be immersed in liquid. Add more water, if needed.
6. Close the lid and let stand at room temperature (about 70°F (20°C)) for 1~2 days. When it smells fermentation, transfer to a refrigerator and preserve.
7. *Kimchi* can be fermented for different lengths of time depending on the flavor preference. Longer fermentation time can produce more sour, more fermented flavor.

Tip

Refer to the *mat-kimchi* section 180p for an easy *kimchi* recipe.
Natural sea salt is used to make *kimchi*. Natural sea salt (sun-dried salt, which is approximately 80% sodium chloride) tastes less salty than *kkot-sogeum* (coarse sea salt) (refined salt, which is approximately 89% sodium chloride) or common table salt (refined salt, which is approximately 99% sodium chloride). However, due to cabbage's high content of minerals such as calcium, cabbages preserved with natural sea salt are crunchy.
In addition to napa cabbages, *kimchi* can be made using various other vegetables. Cabbages and cucumbers, which are popularly used in pickles in other countries, can also be made into *kimchi*.
In Korea, many people have *kimchi* refrigerators that are specially designed to store *kimchi*. When their temperature is configured to an optimal level, a large amount of *kimchi* can be stored for several months. However, stored *kimchi* is generally eaten within two to three weeks.

White Kimchi
Baek-kimchi 백김치

> *Baek-kimchi* is made by stuffing julienned radishes, pears, water parsley and chestnuts between brined napa cabbage leaves and adding *kimchi* liquid. Because *gochut-garu* (red chili pepper powder) is not used, this dish tastes fresh and is not spicy. It is ideal for children or for those who cannot eat spicy food.

Yield 2~3 heads (4 gal, 15kg)

2~3 napa cabbages (about 10 lb, 5kg)
Brine
1 lb (500g) natural sea salt
20 cups (5L) water
Stuffing
¾ white radish (3 lb, 1.5kg)
1 Korean pear (after trimmed 9 oz, 250g)
4 chestnuts
4 jujubes
2 red chili peppers (1 oz, 30g) or ½ oz (15g) red chili pepper threads
10 stalks green onion (3½ oz, 100g)
4 cloves garlic (⅔ oz, 20g)
1 oz (25g) ginger
2 tablespoons salt
Kimchi liquid
½ Korean pear (5 oz, 150g, grated), 8 cups (2L) water, 2½ oz (75g) natural sea salt, ⅓ cup sugar (2 oz, 60g)

Preparation

Brining napa cabbages

1 With a knife, cut the cabbages lengthwise into halves or quarters, depending on sizes.
2 Dissolve the 8 oz (250g) of natural sea salt in 20 cups (5L) of water to make the brine, and soak the cabbage in the brine. Remove the cabbage from the brine and sprinkle with the remaining 8 oz (250g) of natural sea salt evenly between the leaves. In a large container, stack the cabbages neatly and pour the brine over. Let stand for 6-8 hours making sure cabbages stay submerged, use of weight is recommended. Rotate cabbages while soaking from top to bottom.
3 Remove the cabbages from the brine when the leaves have taken in enough salt become limp. Rinse the cabbages thoroughly under running water several times and place cut side down in a colander to drain.

Filling

4 Wash the white radishes clean and peel. Slice crosswise into ¹⁄₁₀-inch (3-mm) thick rounds and then cut into julienne. It is convenient to use a slicer or a grater.
5 Peel the Korean pear and cut into julienne strips the same size as the white radishes.
6 Peel the chestnuts, removing hard outer shell and inner skin, and cut into fine julienne.
7 Remove the seeds of jujubes and cut into fine julienne.
8 Cut the red chili peppers lengthwise in half to remove seeds and slice thinly the red chili peppers on a diagonal. If using red chili pepper threads, cut them into 1-inch (3-cm) long pieces.
9 Wash the green onions and cut into 2-inch (4-cm) long pieces.
10 Cut the garlic and ginger into a fine julienne.

Cooking

1 In a large bowl, combine the strips of white radish, Korean pear, chestnut, jujube, and red chili pepper and toss gently to tint the radish. Add all the prepared filling ingredients; green onions, garlic and ginger. Toss gently with natural sea salt.
2 Insert the stuffing between the leaves of the cabbages. Once filled, wrap the largest outer leaf of the cabbage around filled cabbage. Transfer them into a container and pack up neatly and press them down firmly.
3 In a large bowl, combine the ground pear, natural sea salt, sugar with water and pour into the container containing stuffed cabbage from **2**.
4 Close the lid and let it stand at room temperature (about 70°F (20°C)) for 1-2 days. Once the fermented *kimchi* smell is noticeable, transfer the container to a refrigerator and store it. It will keep for 3 weeks in the refrigerator.

Tip

For a clear *kimchi* liquid of *baek-kimchi*, crushed seasonings are not used.
Because *gochut-garu* (red chili pepper powder) and *jeotgal* (fish sauce) are not used, it is easy for this dish to smell stale. And for that reason, it should be eaten within a short time compared to spicy *kimchi*. Add pear juice for a sweeter and fresher taste.

P4 » P10

C1

C2

C3

Napa Cabbage and Radish Kimchi
Mat-kimchi 맛김치

> *Mat-kimchi* is made by slicing radishes into one-inch squares, brining them in salt and seasoning them with a generous amount of spring onions, garlic and *gochut-garu* (red chili pepper powder). This dish is also called *seokbakji* because it is made by mixing radishes and napa cabbage. Instead of being stored for a long time, it is prepared and served as needed.

Yield 15 gal (6kg)

1 napa cabbage (4 lb, 2kg)
½ white radish (2 lb, 1kg)
9 stalks green onion (3 oz, 90g)

Brine for cabbage
10 oz (300g) natural sea salt
12 cups (3L) water

Brine for radish
2 tablespoons natural sea salt
2 cups water

Seasoning
4 oz (120g) coarse *gochut-garu* (red chili pepper powder),
2 cups water,
2 tablespoons minced garlic,
4 teaspoons minced ginger,
2 tablespoons salt,
4 tablespoons sugar,
4 tablespoons salted shrimp
salt to taste

Preparation

1. Remove the tough or discolored outer leaves of the cabbages. Cut them into 1½-inch (4-cm) long pieces. In a large bowl, dissolve 10oz (300g) natural sea salt in 12 cups (3L) water. Then brine cabbages in it for 2 hours. Rinse the brined cabbages several times and drain in a colander.
2. Cut the radish into 1½×2×¼-inch (3×4×0.5-cm) pieces. In a large bowl, dissolve 2 tablespoons sea salt in 2 cups water. Brine radishes for 2 hours. Rinse the brined radishes several times and drain in a colander.
3. Cut the green onions into 2-inch (4-cm) long pieces.

Cooking

1. In a large bowl, place the cabbages and white radishes and add *gochut-garu*. Toss gently to tint the cabbages and radishes. Add the green onions and rest of the seasoning. Adjust the taste with salt according to your preference.
2. Pack *kimchi* into a container and close the lid tightly. Let it stand at room temperature (about 70°F (20°C)) for 1~2 days. Once the scent of fermenting *kimchi* is noticeable, transfer the container to a refrigerator and store it. It will keep for 3 weeks in the refrigerator.

Tip

Mat-kimchi is easier to make than *baechu-kimchi*.
In Korea, seafood such as oysters and small octopus are added in generous amounts to make a specialty *mat-kimchi* with a savory taste.
Radishes, napa cabbages and other cabbages are often used, but any vegetables may be used with *kimchi* seasoning 45p.

P2

P2

C1

C1

Cucumber Kimchi
Oi-so-bagi 오이소박이

> *Oi-so-bagi* is made by making cuts of cucumber pieces and filling them with chives, garlic and *gochut-garu* (red chili pepper powder).
> This *kimchi* is a summer specialty because of the abundance of cucumbers in summer.

Makes 40

10 English cucumbers (3 lb 7 oz, 1.7kg)
natural sea salt as needed
Brine
13½ oz (400g) natural sea salt
16 cups (4L) water
Stuffing
7 oz (200g) Korean chives
10 tablespoons coarse *gochut-garu* (red chili pepper powder)
1 cup water
4 tablespoons minced green onion
2 tablespoons minced garlic
1 tablespoon minced ginger
1 tablespoon sugar
1 tablespoon salt
Kimchi liquid
1 tablespoon natural sea salt
2 cups water

Preparation

1. Clean each cucumber by rubbing with a little of natural sea salt and then rinse off. Cut into 2-inch (5-cm) long segments. Create pockets in the cucumber, by holding one end of the cucumber on the cutting board, run a small knife through the middle of the cucumber lengthwise, leaving ½-inch (1-cm) uncut at both ends. Turn the cucumber and make another cut through the middle lengthwise to make a cross cut, again leaving ½-inch (1-cm) uncut at both ends. Place them in brine and let them sit for about 2 hours. Weight them down the plate to keep the cucumbers submerged.
2. Remove the cucumbers from the brine and rinse in cold water. Then drain them in a colander.
3. Trim the Korean chives and chop them into ½-inch (1-cm) long pieces.
4. In a bowl, mix the coarse *gochut-garu* and water and let it sit for 10 minutes. Add remaining stuffing ingredients into the bowl and mix well.

Cooking

1. Gently open each pocket by pressing the cucumber's ends with thumb and index finger. Using chopsticks or hands, stuff liberally making sure to fill all 4 slits of each cucumber. Stack them in a jar or an airtight container.
2. To make *kimchi* liquid, add salt and water into the bowl which was used to make stuffing. Pour it over the stuffed cucumber in the container. Then seal the container tightly.
3. Let the container sit at room temperature (about 70°F (20°C)) for a day and store in the refrigerator. It will be ready to eat the next day and will keep for 10 days refrigerated.

Tip

Thick cucumbers are not preferred because seedy cucumbers have a high water content and tend to become mushy easily. It is recommend to use thin pickling cucumbers with thin skins.

P1

P1

P2

P4

C1

Water Kimchi
Nabak-kimchi 나박김치

> *Nabak-kimchi* is made by slicing radishes into thin, square slices, seasoning them with spring onions, garlic and Korean watercress and adding a generous amount of *kimchi* liquid.
> In Korean meals, liquids are essential. Of course, it is proper to serve *guk* (soups), *jjigae* (stews) and *tang* (soups) together; however, during hot summers, chilled *mul-kimchi* such as *nabak-kimchi* (water *kimchi*) may replace hot soup.

Yield 1 gal (5kg)

¼ white radish (1 lb, 500g)
10 oz (300g) napa cabbage hearts
1 teaspoon natural sea salt
1 cup water

Seasoning

1 stalk leek (white part only) (1 oz, 30g), 1 clove garlic (¼ oz, 10g), ⅔ oz (20g) ginger, 1 red chili pepper (½ oz, 15g) (or ⅔ oz (20g) red chili pepper threads), 1⅓ oz (40g) Korean watercress

***Kimchi* liquid**

12 cups (3L) water
2 tablespoons coarse *gochut-garu* (red chili pepper powder)
4 tablespoons natural sea salt
1 tablespoon sugar

Preparation

1. Wash the white radish until exterior is clean. Cut the radish into 1×1-inch (2.5×2.5-cm) squares and then cut into ⅙-inch (0.4-cm) thick.
2. Remove the tough or discolored outside leaves of the cabbages. Cut the cabbage heart lengthwise in half, and then cut into 1×1-inch (3×3-cm) bite sized pieces.
3. Place the radish and cabbages into a big bowl, and sprinkle with the 1 teaspoon natural sea salt and 1 cup of water onto. Let them stand for an hour.
4. Finely julienne the white part of green onion, garlic, and ginger.
5. Halve red chili peppers lengthwise to remove seeds, and then slice diagonally into fine julienne strips. If using red chili pepper threads, cut into 1-inch (3-cm) long pieces.
6. Wash the Korean watercress and cut into 1-inch (3-cm) long pieces.

Cooking

1. In a large bowl, combine the cabbage, radish, Korean watercress, green onion, garlic, ginger and red chili pepper and mix well. Place them into a *kimchi* or plastic container.
2. Pour 12 cups (3L) of water into the bowl that was used to mix the ingredients. Place the *gochut-garu* on cheesecloth or small sieve and secure. Gently swirl the *gochut-garu* pouch in the water to diffuse the color into the water. Then dissolve the natural sea salt and sugar in the liquid to make *kimchi* liquid.
3. Pour *kimchi* liquid into the container full of cut vegetables. Seal the container and leave it out at room temperature (about 70°F (20°C)) for approximately a day, and then store in the refrigerator. It will be ready to eat the follwing day and will keep for 10 days refrigerated.

Tip

Nabak-kimchi is *mul-kimchi* that can be served immediately after making. Chilled *mul-kimchi* is often poured over noodles for the special summer dish.

P3

C1

C2

C3

Radish Water Kimchi
Dongchimi 동치미

> *Dongchimi* is made by pouring a generous amount of brine onto salted radish. Due to their abundance during the Korean winter, white radishes are often preserved. *Dongchimi's* cool and fresh taste goes well with *juk* (porridge) or *tteok* (rice cakes). Well-fermented *dongchimi* liquid can also be poured over *mul-naengmyeon* (buckwheat noodles in chilled broth) 86p. In particular, when well-fermented *dongchimi* liquid is mixed with meat broth, it adds a tangy and fresher taste to the *naengmyeon* broth.

Yield 1 gal (5kg)

½ white radish (for *dongchimi*) (2 lb, 1kg)
1⅔ oz (50g) natural sea salt

Side ingredients
½ Korean pear (10 oz, 300g)
5 stalks green onion (1⅔ oz, 50g)
2 green chili peppers (1 oz, 30g) (fermented with salt, optional)
2 red chili peppers (1 oz, 30g)
3 cloves garlic (½ oz, 15g)
¾ oz (25g) fresh ginger

Glutinous paste
½ tablespoon dried glutinous rice flour
⅓ cup water

***Kimchi* liquid**
8 cups (2L) water
3½ oz (100g) natural sea salt
2 tablespoons sugar
2 tablespoons glutinous paste

Preparation

1. Pick the small and hard white radish. Remove the fine roots and wash the radish with a brush to remove any dirt. Cut the radish into 8 big pieces and coat with 1⅔ oz (50g) salt and let them sit overnight.
2. Wash the Korean pear and cut in half.
3. Wash the green onions. Tie them into 2~3 bundles.
4. Wash the green chili peppers and red chili peppers, and then drain.
5. Wash the garlic and ginger and slice thinly.
6. In a small saucepan, stir the sweet rice flour in water. Bring to a boil and gently cook, stirring constantly with a whisk, until it becomes a paste without lumps. Let it cool.
7. To make the *kimchi* liquid, combine the 2 liters of water, 3½ oz (100g) natural sea salt, 2 tablespoons sugar and 2 tablespoons of glutinous paste, and then mix well.

Cooking

1. Place a layer of salted radishes in a jar, and add the prepared green onions, Korean pear, green chili peppers, red chili peppers, garlic and ginger. Put the remaining radishes on top. Weigh them down with a heavy plate to prevent radishes from floating.
2. Pour the *kimchi* liquid over them and close the lid. Let it sit at room temperature (about 70°F (20°C)) for 2 days until it ferments, and then store in a refrigerator before serving.
3. For serving, take out the radishes and cut into half-moon shape, or slice into ½×½×1½-inch (1×1×4-cm) thick pieces. Cut the green onions, pear and chili peppers into small pieces. Adjust the taste of the fermented brine with water or sugar, if necessary.

Tip

Although *dongchimi* takes a considerable amount of time to ferment if it is made using whole winter radishes, it can be stored for a long period. To prepare more quickly, make *dongchimi* with radish pieces.
Add fermented peppers with salt and *cheonggak* (seaweed) to *dongchimi* for a savory taste.

P1

P2 » P5

P6

C2

C2

Desserts

Tteok (rice cake) and *hangwa* (Korean traditional confectionery)
are representative desserts in Korea.
Rice cake refers to powdered grain, steamed and molded into various shapes.
Most rice cakes are made of short-grain or glutinous rice. Korean traditional confectionery
refers to traditional sweets made with grains and fruits, honey and sugar.
Eumryo (drinks) are generally categorized into *hwachae* (chilled punch) or
cha (hot or brewed tea) according to the temperature.

Half-moon Rice Cakes

Songpyeon 송편

> This rice cake is made by kneading non-glutinous rice flour with boiling water, filling the dough with sesame seeds, beans or red beans, forming it into scalloped shapes and steaming it on pine needles. Because grains are staple ingredients in Korea, there are many types of rice cakes. Rice cakes can be cooked for meals, such as *tteokguk* (sliced rice cake soup) 96p and *tteok-bokki* (stir-fried rice cakes with gochu-jang sauce) 72p, or may be eaten as desserts, such as *injeolmi* (glutinous rice cake coated with bean flour) and *hwajeon*. In particular, rice cakes are an essential part of the menu at Korean family gatherings. *Songpyeon* is made on *Chuseok* to thank the ancestors and heaven for the fresh-fruit and grain harvests. *Chuseok* falls on August 15 according to the lunar calendar, and its meaning is similar to that of Thanksgiving Day.

Makes 16

Dough
2 cups short-grain rice flour*
(8 oz, 240g)
1 cup boiling water

Sesame Filling
½ cup sesame seeds (1½ oz, 45g)
⅛ cup honey (1⅔ oz, 50g) or 1 tablespoon sugar

Bean Filling
1 cup fresh black beans (7 oz, 200g) (or ½ cup dried black beans (3½ oz, 100g))
⅓ teaspoon salt

pine needles, sesame oil as needed

*****Preparation
for short-grain rice flour
Soak 1 cup (8 oz, 225g) of short-grain rice in 2 cups of cold water overnight. Drain them using a sieve and let stand on the sieve for 30 minutes. Then, add 1½ tablespoons of water and grind them finely.

Preparation

1 Add boiling water to the rice flour and knead well until smooth dough forms. Let the dough rest in a plastic bag for 30 minutes.
2 To make the sesame filling, toast the sesame seeds in a frying pan or oven and crush. Mix them with honey to form paste.
3 To make the bean filling, mix beans with salt. When using dried beans, rehydrate before using.
4 Separate the pine needles from the branches and get rid of black tips. Rinse well and drain in a colander.

Cooking

1 Make balls out of a small piece of the dough about the size of a chestnut.
2 Using your thumb, press gently in the middle of the doughball to form a well or depression, and fill them with sesame filling or bean filling using a spoon. Seal the well making sure filling doesn't leak out and mold into a shell or half-moon shape.
3 Spread fresh pine needles on the bottom of the steamer. Place *songpyeons* (half-moon rice cakes) on the pine needles and arrange fresh pine needles between layers of *songpyeons* so they are not touching each other.
4 Steam *songpyeons* for 30 minutes until they are cooked well. Remove *songpyeons* from the steamer.
5 Gently remove pine needles from *songpyeons*. Add sesame oil and toss to coat *songpyeons*. Place them in a serving plate.

Tip

A subtle scent of pine needles from the steamer on which *songpyeons* are steamed is this dish's appealing point. However, when pine needles are unavailable, a steamer with wet cotton cloths may be used. Coloring ingredients such as mugwort is added to the rice flour.

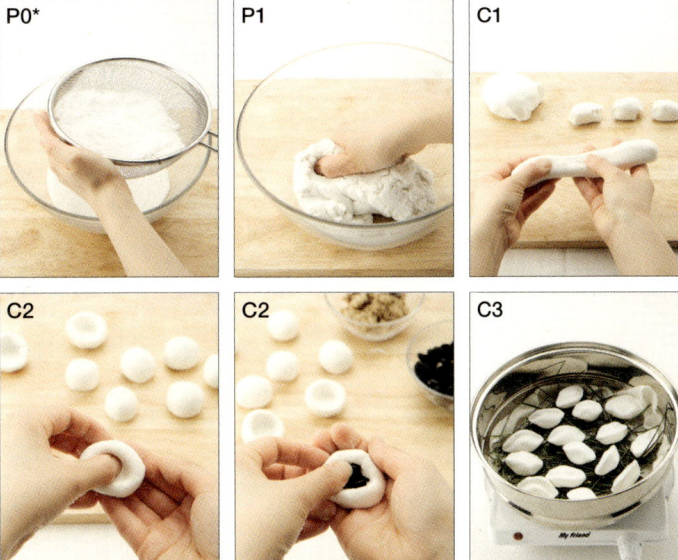

Flower Rice Cakes
Hwajeon 화전

> *Hwajeon* is made by kneading glutinous rice flour with boiling water, forming flat, round shapes, pan-frying them in oil and garnishing them with flower petals. This traditional food expresses nature in its four seasons. In Korea, seasonal edible flower petals are used. Azaleas in spring, roses in summer and chrysanthemums in autumn are used as garnishes.

Makes 12~16

Dried glutinous rice flour, Makes 12
2 cups dried glutinous rice flour (½ lb 7 oz, 320g)
½ teaspoon salt
12 tablespoons cold water

Wet glutinous rice flour, Makes 16
2 cups (8 oz, 240g) wet glutinous rice flour*
½ teaspoon salt
4 tablespoons boiling water

12 edible flowers (azalea, rose, chrysanthemum, etc.)
sugar or honey as needed
vegetable oil as needed

*Preparation for wet glutinous rice flour
Soak 1 cup (8 oz, 225g) of glutinous rice in 2 cups of cold water overnight. Drain them using a sieve and let stand on the sieve for 30 minutes. Then grind them finely.

Preparation

1 Place the dried sweet rice flour in a large bowl. In a small bowl, dissolve the salt in boiling water. Add it into the glutinous rice flour little by little, and knead well by hands until the dough is smooth. Keep the dough in a plastic bag for 20 minutes. When using the wet glutinous rice flour, use cold water.
2 Break off chestnut-sized pieces of dough and mold into round and flat shapes 2-inch (5-cm) diameter.
3 Prepare edible petals as a garnish. Remove a stamen and wash, and then dry with a paper towel.

Cooking

1 Heat a skillet over high heat and add vegetable oil. Once it's heated up, reduce the heat to very low. Put the rice doughs on the skillet, preventing from sticking together, and cook them. When the bottoms become transparent, flip them over with a spatula and cook for a few minutes.
2 Decorate the top with the petals.
3 When both sides are cooked, coat them with the sugar or honey evenly.

Tip

Any types of thin edible flower petals may be used as a garnish. Adjust the amount of water according to the type of glutinous rice flour, whether it is dry processed or wet.

P1

P1

P2

C2

Twisted Honey Cookies
Maejakgwa 매작과

> This traditional Korean pastry is made by thinly rolling flour dough with ginger juice, frying it in oil and dipping it in honey. This sweet fried and honey glazed pastry, *maejakgwa* has simple ingredients and is easy to make.

Makes 40

1 cup (120g) all-purpose flour
½ teaspoon salt
½ oz (15g) fresh ginger
3 tablespoons water
vegetable oil as needed
2 tablespoons pine nuts
all-purpose flour as needed for kneading

Syrup for dipping
1 cup sugar (200g), 1 cup water (240ml), 2 tablespoons honey (or corn syrup),
¼ teaspoon cinnamon powder

Preparation

1. Sift the flour and salt together into a large bowl.
2. Peel the ginger and grate. Extract the ginger juice by placing the grated ginger on a strainer and then pressing it down with a tablespoon. It can also be done by using cheesecloth.
3. Add the ginger juice and water into the flour and knead well with hands. Put the dough in a plastic bag and set it aside for 30 minutes.
4. To make syrup, place 1 cup sugar and 1 cup water into a saucepan and bring to a boil over medium heat and do not stir. When the sugar is dissolved, reduce the heat to low and add the honey or corn syrup, and simmer for 10 more minutes, until it is reduced to 1 cup. Remove the syrup from heat and let it cool. Add cinnamon powder into the dipping syrup and stir well.
5. Remove the pine nut tips. Chop the pine nuts finely with a knife on a paper or grind them with a rotary cheese grater.

Cooking

1. Take the dough out from the plastic bag and roll it out with a rolling pin on a floured work surface into as thin as 1/16-inch (1-mm) thick sheet. Cut the sheets of cookie dough into 2×1-inch (5×2-cm) rectangles, dusting the sheets with extra flour often to avoid sticking.
2. Make 3 slits lengthwise in the middle of each piece of dough. The middle slit should be a little bit longer than others. Push one end of the dough through the center slit to make a ribbon shape.
3. Heat the vegetable oil until it reaches 330°F (160°C) in a wok or frying pan. Deep-fry the dough until crispy and golden brown. Lift the cookies out of the oil and drain on paper towels.
4. Dip the cookies in the syrup to lightly coat them and drain off the excess syrup.
5. Place the cookies on a serving plate and sprinkle with the powdered pine nuts evenly on top.

Tip

Sometimes, colorants and flavors are added when kneading the flour dough.

Ginger and Cinnamon Punch
Sujeonggwa 수정과

> This beverage is made by adding sugar or honey to a brew of cinnamon and ginger and is chilled before being served. Soaked *gotgam* (dried persimmons) and pine nuts are used to garnish the drink. Served icy cold with soft dried persimmons, this drink is a delicacy during the cold winter.

Serves 8~10

Ginger liquid
2 oz (60g) fresh ginger
6 cups water

Cinnamon liquid
1½ oz (45g) cinnamon sticks
6 cups water

4 dried persimmons (7 oz, 200g)
1 cup brown sugar (7 oz, 200g)
1 tablespoon pine nuts

Preparation

1. Peel the ginger and slice thinly.
2. Break the cinnamon sticks into small pieces and rinse in water.
3. Remove the stems of dried persimmons and make them into round shapes by hands.
4. Remove the pine nut tips and wipe with a paper towel.

Cooking

1. In a large saucepan, put ginger slices and water and bring to a boil over high heat. When it begins to boil, reduce the heat to low and simmer for 30 minutes. Strain it through a colander lined with cheesecloth. Reserve the liquid.
2. In another large saucepan, put cinnamon sticks and water and bring to a boil over high heat. When it begins to boil, reduce the heat to low and simmer for 40 minutes. Strain it through a colander, lined with cheesecloth. Reserve the liquid.
3. In a large pot, combine the reserved ginger and cinnamon-boiled water and add brown sugar. Bring back to a boil over low heat for 10 minutes. Remove the pot from the heat and let it cool.
4. Place the dried persimmons in a punch bowl and pour the chilled punch. Serve with a few pine nuts floating on top.

Tip

It is preferable to use half-dried persimmons. To make the dried persimmons softer, soak them in the beverage in advance. If dried persimmons are unavailable, pine nuts may be floated in the beverage. Although *sujeonggwa* is often served chilled, it may be served hot.

If cinamon sticks boil over high heat continously, the bitterness of the cinnamon will come out into the liquid and make it not useable.

P1 » P4

C1 » C2

C3

Omija Punch
Omija-hwachae 오미자화채

> This cold beverage is made by brewing dried *omija* and adding sugar or honey. In the springtime, it is often garnished with azalea petals or served on a flower-shaped boat.
> '*Omija*' means a fruit with five tastes (sweet, sour, bitter, salty and spicy). And *hwachae* means cold beverages made from fruit juice, honey water or *omija* brewed with a garnish. Although *omija-hwachae* is a cold beverage, it may be enjoyed all year round. *Omija-hwachae* tastes like cranberry juice, and the most popular juice used to make it is an *omija* brew. Garnish the sweet and sour *omija* brew with seasonal fruits or edible flowers to enjoy the taste of the season.

Serves 8~10

2 oz (60g) dried *omija* (Schisandra)
6 cups water
1 cup sugar (7 oz, 200g)
¼ Korean pear (5 oz, 150g)

Preparation

1. Wash dried *omija* and soak them in 2 cups of cold water overnight. Strain through a very fine strainer lined with cheesecloth. Reserve the liquid.
2. To make a punch, add 4 cups water and sugar to the *omija*-soaked water. Stir it to dissolve the sugar. Keep it in a refrigerator.
3. Cut the Korean pear into fine julienne, or cut it out with a small flower-shaped cutter.

Cooking

1. Pour the punch into a punch bowl, serve with pears floating on top.

Tip

Although dried *omija* is hard to find, once obtained in a generous amount, it can be stored in the freezer for a long time. Good *omija* has rich flesh, a vivid color and a sticky texture.

P1

P2

Yuja Punch
Yuja-hwachae 유자화채

> This cold beverage is made by adding finely julienned *yuja* peels and pears to *yuja* juice and garnishing it with pomegranate seeds.
> The unique flavor of *yuja* complements the sweet and fresh taste of pears. Pomegranate seeds are used to garnish the drink for a color and taste.

Serves 8

1 *yuja* (4 oz, 120g)
½ Korean pear (10 oz, 300g)
2 tablespoons pomegranate seeds

Punch liquid
4 cups water
1 cup sugar (7 oz, 200g) sugar

Preparation

1 Cut the *yuja* into four pieces and cut away the peel along the curvature of the fruit. Place the peel on a cutting board, slice off the inner white part of the skin and cut the yellow peel and inner white peel into fine julienned strips separately.
2 Wrap the peeled fruit in clean cheesecloth and squeeze juice out.
3 Peel the pear and cut into fine julienne.
4 With thumbs, remove the pomegranate seeds gently.
5 Dissolve the sugar well in water in a large bowl. Mix in the *yuja* juice to make punch liquid.

Cooking

1 In a punch bowl, arrange the *yuja* strips and pear strips side by side.
2 Gently pour the punch liquid and set aside for 30 minutes to infuse the *yuja* flavor in a refrigerator.
3 Garnish with pomegranate seeds.

Tip

In other countries, it is difficult to find fresh *yuja*, which can be replaced with the preserved *yuja* in sugar found in the tea section of Asian grocery stores. The is convenient because it can be served after adding either cold or hot water.

P1

P4

P1 » P4

P5

Setting the Korean Table

CHAPTER 1
The Traditional Korean Table Setting

The *sangcharim* (Korean table setting) refers to the arrangement of main and side dishes on a single table. Depending on the person's social or economic status, the table (*bansang*) can be referred to as *surasang* for the royal court, *jinjisang* for the nobles, and *bapsang* for common people. Also the number and amount of food served varies as well depending on their statues.

1 Principles of Bansang Preparation

It is traditional to prepare the *sangcharim* as *doksang* or *oesang* (table setting for a single person). Generally, a *bapsang* consists of *bap* (cooked rice), *guk* (soups), *kimchi*, *cheongjang* or *guk-ganjang* (soy sauce for soup) and 3, 5, 7, 9-odd numbers of *banchan* (side dishes). Typically, 5 side dishes are served with *jjiae* (stews) and 7 side dishes are served with *jjim* (steamed dishes) or *jorim* (braised dishes). Seasonings such as *cho-ganjang* (soy sauce with vinegar), *cho-gochu-jang* (red chili pepper paste with vinegar) or mustard sauce are served with *jeon* (pan-fried dishes) or *pyeonyuk* (slices of boiled meat). Beside the odd number of side dishes, two or three additional types of *kimchi* are added to the table setting as well.

Side dishes are selected based on the season, and each is prepared with unique ingredients and cooking methods in no duplication. A *bansang* prepared using these principles that described below not only satisfies the appetite, but provides ample nutrition.

How to arrange the oesang (table setting for single person)

Place the spoon and chopsticks horizontally on the right side of the table. Arrange the spoon in front of the chopsticks with the handles hanging 1-inch (3-cm) from the edge of the table. Place the *bap* (cooked rice) on the left, the *guk* (broth) on the right and the *jjim* (steamed dishes) behind the *guk* (broth) in the nearest row on the table to the diner. Serve the *ganjang* (soy sauce), *cho-gochu-jang* (red chili pepper paste with vinegar) and *cho-ganjang* (soy sauce with vinegar) in the second row. Next, place the *jaengcheop* (small

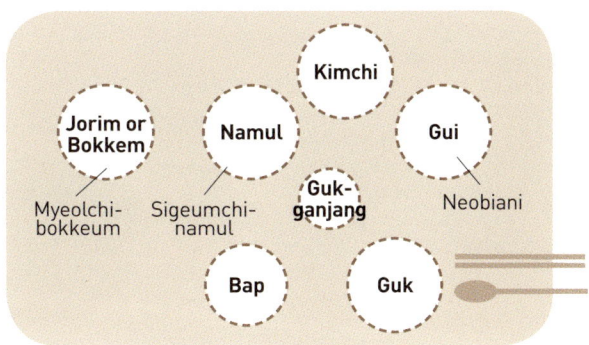

Example of a 3-cheop bansang

bowl) do not have a set position, but are recommended to be placed behind sauce bowls in the third row. Salty side dishes such as *jangajji* (pickled vegetables) or *jeotgal* (salted fish) should be placed on the left, ordinary side dishes such as cooked or fresh vegetables in the middle and hot fries or specialdishes on the right.

2 Unique Korean Kitchenwares

The following list introduces the kitchenwares and equipment used to store and cook food and the ordinary *bansang* tablewares.

Bansanggi

The set of dishes used for the *bansang*, including *jubal* (rice bowl), *tanggi* (broth bowl), *jochibo* (stew bowl), *bosigi* (kimchi bowl), *jongji* (small bowl for sauces such as soy sauce with vinegar, red chili pepper paste with vinegar and honey) and *jaengcheop* (small bowl for other side dishes such as *jeon* (pan-fried dishes), *gui* (grilled dishes), *namul* (seasoned vegetables) and *jangajji* (pickled vegetables). Dishes have lids and are made of wood, brass, silver and porcelain. Koreans use different tableware for each season. For example, brass is often used in the winter to keep the food warm, and white porcelain is used in the summer for its cool freshness.

Ceramics Earthenware and porcelain dishes. These dishes are made with good clay enamel-coated, painted, and baked at a high temperature. Porcelain is stronger than earthenware and is sealed with an enamel coating. Porcelain may be white with pale blue or blue with a beautiful celadon green accents.

Brassware Dishes made of brass by casting or forging. Brassware was primarily used in the royal court or by nobles to keep the food warm, cool, or for hygienic purposes. It is not used as ordinary tableware because it is expensive and hard to clean. However, the excellence and beauty of brassware is highlighted in traditional Korean restaurants or dessert cafes.

Pottery Earthen vessels made of red clay (baked without enamel) and crockery (earthen vessels painted with enamel and re-baked). Household pottery includes the jars used to store pastes, *kimchi* and liquor and the small, fat pots used to store *gochu-jang* (red chili pepper paste), *kimchi*, liquor, vinegar, salted fish and pickled vegetables. Another type of jar, the *ttukbaegi* (earthen pot), is a strong, fire-resistant crock used to boil and serve stew. It is used to boil *tangban* (rice in broth), such as *seolleong-tang* (OX bone soup) and *jangguk-bap* (rice served in beef soup), directly over an open fire.

Cast iron (iron) Iron cauldrons are thick, multi-purpose vessels with heavy lids used to cook rice or broth.The *beoncheol (frying pan)* used to fry *jeon* or *jijim* (pan-fried dishes) is round and flat.

Dolsot (stone pot) A pot made of talc. The pot is round and is primarily used to cook *yakbap* (glutinous rice with nuts and jujubes) and *chalbap* (cooked glutinous rice). It cooks the rice evenly and can keep the rice warm without burning it. Its even warmth is ideal for making *dolsot bibimbap* (*bibimbap* served in a stone pot) or *jeongol* (hot pot).

Wood Dishes made of wood. Wooden containers include *jegi* (wooden vessel for ancestral rites) and *gujeol-pan* (platter of nine delicacies).

Sinseollo

This is a royal hot pot with a charcoal brazier and served directly on the table. It is used to boil the food while eating. The hot pot is round with a 4~8-inch (12~24-cm)-diameter. It also has a 2~3-inch (6~9-cm) cylinder in the center in which charcoal is placed and around which the food to be eaten is arranged. It delivers both practical and beautiful dining experience.

Gujeol-pan

Gujeol-pan is the name of the vessel that lends itself to the name of the dish. An octagonal wooden vessel partitioned into 9 sections: 8 around the edge and 1 in the center. The vessel is used to serve *gujeol-pan* (platter of nine delicacies), with *mil-jeonbyeong* (thin wheat wrapper) in the center surrounded by side dishes. Also, dried snacks, stewed fruit or fruits preserved in honey can be served in this plate.

1 Bansang Charim
4 Bibimbap Sangcharim

CHAPTER 2
Korean Menu Suggestion

This chapter presents diverse meals utilize already introduced recipes in this book. Considering ideal taste and nutrients, the foods can be proudly served for any time and situation.

1 Bansang Charim (Korean Style Table Setting)

This setting is the basic form of Korean table setting, and it is important to balance various ingredients and cooking methods for the harmony of taste and nutrition. Basically there are *bap* (cooked rice), *guk* (soups) or *jjigae* (stews) and *kimchi* as well as three kinds of *banchan* (side dishes). There should be both hot and cold food, food with soup and without soup, spicy food and non-spicy food, and meat and vegetables evenly.

Huin-bap (Cooked White Rice) 78p
Sigeumchi-doenjang-guk (Spinach Soybean Paste Soup) 102p
Baechu-kimchi (Whole Cabbage Kimchi) 174p
Saengseon-gui (Grilled Fish) 128p
Dubu-jorim (Braised Dubu in Soy Sauce) 152p
Kong-namul-muchim (Seasoned Bean Sprouts) 64p

Ogok-bap (Cooked Five-Grain Rice) 78p
Sundubu-jjigae (Spicy Soft Dubu Stew) 54p
Back-kimchi (White Kimchi) 178p
Neobiani (Grilled Marinated beef Slices) 118p
Myeolchi-bokkeum (Stir-fried Dried Anchovy) 158p
Sigeumchi-namul (Seasoned Spinach) 164p

2 Juksang Charim (Porridge Table Setting)

Juk (porridge) is for enjoying delicacy or for when you are sick. Mild side dishes that are easy to digest should be set with porridge.

Hobak-juk (Pumpkin Porridge) 82p
Nabak-kimchi (Water Kimchi) 184p
Tangpyeong-chae (Mung Bean Jelly mixed with Vegetables) 142p
Gyeran-jjim (Steamed Eggs) 168p

3 Myeonsang Charim (Noodles Table Setting)

There are noodle dishes that have soup, such as *janchi-guksu* (noodles in anchovy broth) 90p and *mul-naengmyeon* (buckwheat noodles in chilled broth) 86p, and that don't have soup, such as *goldong-myeon* (noodles mixed with vegetables and beef) 92p and *bibim-naengmyeon* (spicy buckwheat noodles) 88p. And it can also vary in temperature from warm noodles; *on-myeon*, and cold noodles; *naengmyeon*. Noodles are mostly of carbohydrate so proteins, such as meat and eggs, are served with noodles.

Janchi-guksu / On-myeon (Noodles in Anchovy Broth) 90p
Baechu-kimchi (Whole Cabbage Kimchi) 178p
Pyeonyuk (Slices of Boiled Meat) 122p

Goldong-myeon / Bibim-guksu (Noodles mixed with Vegetables and Beef) 92p
Nabak-kimchi (Water Kimchi) 184p
Gyeran-mari (Rolled Omelet) 170p

Mul-naengmyeon (Buckwheat Noodles in Chilled Broth) 86p
Dongchimi (Radish Water Kimchi) 186p
Galbi-gui (Grilled Beef Short Ribs) 120p

Bibim-naengmyeon (Spicy Buckwheat Noodles) 88p
Oi-naengguk (Chilled Cucumber Soup) 104p
Salmeun-Gyeran (Boiled Eggs)

4 Bibimbap Sangcharim (Bibimbap Table Setting)

It is a one-dish food with cooked white rice and various vegetables. It is very nutritious, and also convenient to eat. Clear soup or watery *kimchi* is served with *bibimbap*. *Dubu* (tofu) can be used in the place of meat for vegetarians diners as well.

Bibimbap (Rice Mixed with Vegetables and Beef) 52p
Kong-namul-guk (Bean Sprouts Soup)
Dongchimi (Radish Water Kimchi) 186p

5 Bossam Sangcharim (Boiled Pork Wrapped with Napa Cabbage Table Setting)

It is a one-dish meal consists of boiled pork and *baechu-kimchi* (whole cabbage kimchi). The taste and nutrition of the meat and vegetables compliments each other. A tradition in Korean, people make a year's supply of *kimchi* on November, and they always have this boiled pork on the day of *kimchi*-making.

Dwaeji-bossam (Boiled Pork Wrapped with Napa Cabbage) 122p
Baechu-geot-jeori (Fresh Kimchi) 162p
   or Baechu-kimchi (Whole Cabbage Kimchi) 174p
Nokdu-bindae-tteok (Mung Bean Pancake) 132p

6 Sangchu-ssam Sangcharim (Lettuce Wraps Table Setting)

It is a hearty and nutritious meal of wrapped *bap* (cooked rice) and/or meat in a vegetable leaf.

Sangchu-ssam (Lettuce-wraps)
   - Sanchu (Lettuce), Ssukgat (Crown daisy), Putgochu (Green chili pepper)
Bap (Cooked Rice) 78p
Doenjang-jjigae (Soybean Paste Stew) 106p
   or Ssam-jang (Seasoned Soybean Paste) 46p
Bulgogi (Grilled Marinated Beef) 58p
   or Dwaeji-bulgogi / Jeyuk-bokkeum (Spicy Stir-fried Pork) 62p

7 Dagwasang Charim (Tea Table Setting)

This setting is for serving desserts or tea time. Refreshments like *tteok* (rice cake), *hangwa* (Korean traditional confectionary) and/or seasonal fruits are served in this setting. Warm teas, such as green tea, or cold drinks, such as *omija hwachae* (*omija* punch) and *sujeonggwa* (ginger and cinnamon punch) 196p, are served with the desserts.

Songpyeon (Half-moon Rice Cakes) 190p
Maejakgwa (Twisted Honey Cookies) 194p
Sujeonggwa (Ginger and Cinnamon Punch) 196p

6 Sangchu-ssam Sangcharim   7 Dagwasang Charim

Hwajeon (Flower Rice Cakes) 192p
Omija-hwachae (Omija Punch) 198p
    or Yuja-hwachae (Yuja Punch) 200p

8 Juansang Charim (Liquor Table Setting)

Traditional liquor and foods such as *sinseollo* (royal hot pot) or *gujeol-pan* (platter of nine delicacies) are served in the liquor table setting. Recently, commercial liquors such as *makgeolli* (unrefined rice wine), *soju* (Korean distilled liquor), and *maekju* (beer) are served along with traditional liquors. Matching foods according to the type of liquor are suggested below.

Jeontong-ju (Traditional liquor)
      - Yakju (Clear rice wine), Malgeun-sul (Refined rice wine), Bizeun-sul (Brewed liquor)
Sinseollo (Royal hot pot)
Gujeol-pan (Platter of Nine Delicacies) 138p
Neobiani (Grilled Marinated Beef Slices) 118p
Modum-jeon (Assorted Savory Pancakes) 64p
Tangpyeong-chae (Mung Bean Jelly Mixed with Vegetables) 142p

Makgeolli (Unrefined rice wine)
Haemul-pajeon (Seafood and Green Onion Pancake) 66p
    or Kimchi-jeon (Kimchi Pancake), Nokdu-bindae-tteok (Mung Bean Pancake) 132p
Dubu-kimchi (Dubu with Stir-fried Kimchi) 154p
Gyeran-jjim (Steamed Eggs) 168p
Mat-kimchi (Napa Cabbage and Radish Kimchi) 186p

Soju (Korean distilled liquor)
Dak-bokkeum-tang (Spicy Braised Chicken) 126p
Gyeran-jjim (Steamed Eggs) 168p
Dongchimi (Radish Water Kimchi) 186p

Maekju (Beer)
Maekom-dak-gangjeong (Deep-fried Chicken with Sweet and Spicy Sauce) 74p

9 Potluck Party
Potluck party is an opportunity to freely show each other's cooking styles and abilities. Participating people discusses what to bring among meats, vegetables, main dishes (cooked rice, noodles, dumplings), side dishes, and special dishes so that nobody brings the same kind of food.

Gimbap (Toasted Laver Rolls) 70p
Tteok-bokki (Stir-fried Rice Cakes with Gochu-jang Sauce) 72p
    or Gungjung-tteok-bokki (Royal Stir-fried Rice Cakes) 144p
Japchae (Stir-fried Sweet Potato Noodles and Vegetables) 68p
Maekom-dak-gangjeong (Deep-fried Chicken with Sweet and Spicy Sauce) 74p

Ogok-bap (Cooked Five-grain Rice) 78p
Bulgogi (Grilled Marinated Beef) 58p
Gujeol-pan (Platter of Nine Delicacies) 138p
Ojingeo-bokkeum (Spicy Stir-fried Squid) 130p
Modum-Jeon (Assorted Savory Pancakes) 64p
Sangchu-oi-saengchae (Lettuce Salad with Cucumber) 160p

10 Myeongjeol Sangcharim (Special Holiday Table Setting)
Traditionally, there are special kinds of seasonal foods for holidays. All of them are prepared by using seasonal ingredients.

1) Seollal (Lunar New Year's Day)
Tteokguk (Sliced Rice Cake Soup) 96p
Galbi-gui (Grilled Beef Short Ribs) 120p
Baechu-kimchi (Whole Cabbage Kimchi) 174p
Samsaek-namul (Three-colored Seasoned Vegetables) 164p
Sujeonggwa (Ginger and Cinnamon Punch) 196p
Gyejeol-gwail (Seasonal fruits)

2) Jeongwol Daeboreum (First Full Moon)
Ogok-bap (Cooked Five-grain Rice) 78p
Gim-gui (Toasted Laver)
Sigeumchi-doenjang-guk (Spinach Soybean Paste Soup) 102p
Baek-kimchi (White Kimchi) 178p
Beoseot-namul (Seasoned Mushrooms) 164p
    or Gosari-namul (Seasoned Bracken) 166p
Gogi-jeon (Pan-fried Beef Cakes) 64p
Maejakgwa (Twisted Honey Cookies) 194p
Yaksik (Glutinous Rice with Nuts and Jujubes)
Bureom (Nuts)

9 Potluck Party

3) Boknal (The Hottest Days of Summer)
Samgye-tang (Ginseng Chicken Soup) or Yukgaejang (Spicy Beef Soup) 114,112p
Huin-bap (Cooked White Rice) 78p
Oi-so-bagi (Cucumber Kimchi) 182p
Omija-hwachae (Omija Punch) 198p
Gyejeol-gwail (Seasonal Fruits)

4) Chuseok (Harvest Festival)
Songpyeon (Half-moon Rice Cakes) 190p
Japchae (Stir-fried Sweet Potato Noodles and Vegetables) 68p
Neobiani (Grilled Marinated Beef Slices) 118p
So-gogi-beoseot-jeongol (Beef and Mushroom Hot Pot) 110p
Nabak-kimchi (Water Kimchi) 184p
Nokdu-bindae-tteok (Mung Bean Pancake) 132p
Gyejeol-gwail (Seasonal Fruits)

5) Dongji (Winter Solstice)
Patjuk (Red Bean Porridge)
    with Saealsim (Balls made from glutinous rice flour) 84p
Dongchimi (Radish Water Kimchi) 186p
Yuja-hwachae (Yuja Punch) 200p
Gyejeol-gwail (Seasonal Fruits)

CHAPTER 3
How to Enjoy Korean Food

This chapter introduces the proper way to eat Korean food on one table setting unlike course meal of Western food, and also how to use a spoon and chopsticks without troubles.

1 General Table Manners

Typical Korean dining table is called *bapsang* or *bansang* (literally 'rice table'), in which side dishes are served with a bowl of *bap* (cooked rice) 78p. The basic bap of *bansang* is not seasoned because it is eaten with other foods that are seasoned such as soup and side dishes.

- *Sujeo* (spoon and chopsticks) literally refer to the set of spoon and chopsticks.
- Both the spoon and chopsticks are used when eating Korean food.
- Spoon is for rice and soup, and chopsticks are for picking up side dishes.
- Spoon and chopsticks are not held in both hands nor should they be held together in one hand.
- For setting spoon and chopsticks on the table, when setting them vertically, the spoon goes on the left and chopsticks go on the right side of the spoon, and when setting them horizontally, they should be put on the right side of the soup, and the chopstick goes above the spoon.
- Eating alone, when facing the table the rice bowl goes on the left hand side, and the soup goes on the right hand side. Side dishes are laid behind the rice bowl and the soup.
- When more than one person is eating together, the bowl of rice and soup is served in an individual bowl. Unlike rice and soup, the side dishes are served in large plates on the center of table. People help themselves on individual plates in a family style serving.

2 Eating Ssam (Wraps)

Ssam is eating *bap* (cooked rice) or meat wrapped in leaf vegetables, laver or wheat crepes in one bite. Type of vegetables to make your wrap and ingredients to put in can be anything of your choosing.

- When eating a lettuce wrap, first you hold a piece of lettuce which is inverted on your hand and put cooked rice and/or meat on it.
- You can also put various vegetables in layers or strong flavor herbs such as garlic and spring onions in the wrap. *Ssam-jang* (seasoned soybean paste) or *gochu-jang* (red chili pepper paste) are also added in the *ssam*.
- When making a wrap with *mil-jeonbyeong* (wheat crepes) in *gujeol-pan* (platters of nine delicacies) you put one crepe on a plate and put 2~3 ingredients at a time rather than putting all 8 ingredients, and add small amount of *cho-ganjang* (soy sauce with vinegar) or *gyeoja-jang* (mustard sauce), then roll the crepe and enjoy.

3 Mixing Bibimbap

Bibimbap 52p is a dish in which different kinds of vegetables and meat are placed on a bowl of *bap* (cooked rice) and *gochu-jang* (red chili pepper paste) is served in a separate bowl. There is no strict rule for the ingredients in *bibimbap*, but usually ingredients in the five cardinal colors of traditional Korean art (white, black, yellow, red and green) are used.

- The bowl for serving *bibimbap* should be a large and wide one like a salad bowl so the food won't overflow outside of the bowl while mixing.
- Spoon is usually used to mix the ingredients of *bibimbap*. However, you can also use chopsticks to prevent the rice being mashed and vegetables being lumped.
- Sweet and spicy *yak-gochu-jang* (seasoned red chili pepper paste) 47p made with ground meat, honey and sesame oil or *ssam-jang* (seasoned soybean paste) 46p, or seasoned *ganjang* (soy sauce) are sometimes added instead of *gochu-jang* according to taste.

References

- Bibigo. (2014). *Healthy & Fresh Korean Kitchen*. Seoul: Postpaper.
- Bittman, M. (2012). *How to Cook Everything the basics: all you need to make great food*. Boston, MA: Houghton Mifflin Harcourt.
- Cecilia, L. H. J. (2005). *Eating Korean: from Barbecue to Kimchi, Recipes from My Home*. Boston, MA: Houghton Mifflin Harcourt.
- Chang, S. Y. (1997). *A Korean Mother's Cooking Note*. Seoul: Ewha Womans University Press.
- Chronicle Books. (2009). *Quick and Easy Korean Cooking*. San Francisco, CA: Chronicle Books.
- Chun, L., Massov, O. (2012). *The Kimchi Cookbook: 60 Traditional and Modern Ways to Make and Eat Kimchi*. New York, NY: Ten Speed Press.
- Chung, H. K. (2009). *Korean Cuisine A cultural Journey*. Seoul: Thinking Tree Publishing.
- Chung, S. Y. (2002). *Korean Cooking*. North Clarendon, VT: Periplus Editions Ltd.
- Chung, S. Y. (2007). *Korean Cooking Made Easy: Simple Meals in Minutes*. North Clarendon, VT: Tuttle Publishing.
- Cooking Penguin. (2013). *Mashitta! A Collection of Simple South Korean Recipes (Black & White)*. North Charleston, SC: Createspace Independent Publishing Platform.
- Dong-A Ilbo. (2010). *Korean Food, The Impression and the Originality*. Seoul: Dong-A Ilbo.
- Freeland-Graves, J. H., Peckham, G. C. (1996). *Foundations of Food Preparation, Sixth Edition*. Englewood Cliffs, NJ: Prentice-Hall, Inc.
- Gisslen, W. (2003). *Professional cooking, Fifth Edition*. Somerset, NJ: John Wiley & Sons, Inc.
- Han, B. J. (2011). *Korean Cooking technique Ⅰ: Korean Utensils and Ingredients*『한식조리기술 총서, 한식 조리도구와 식품재료』. Jeonju: Jeonju University.
- Han, B. J., Han. B. R. (1998). *We must know Korean Food 100 variety*『우리가 정말 알아야 할 우리 음식 백 가지』. Seoul: Hyeonamsa.
- Han, B. R. (2004). *Royal Cuisine of The Joseon Dynasty*『조선왕조 궁중음식』. *Institute of Korean Royal Cuisine*. Seoul: Hwasanmunhwa
- Han, B. S. (2009). *Han, Boksun's Korean Food*『한복선의 우리 음식』. Seoul: Leescom Publishing.
- Happiness of Korean Food. (2010). *The Happiness of Korean Food*. Seoul: Story Blossom.
- Heo, H. (2012). *Familiar Korean Cooking by young chef*. Seoul: Hyegiwon.
- Hwang, H. S., Han, B. R., Chung, G. J. (2003). *Carry on Royal Cuisine of The Joseon Dynasty*『황혜성 한복려

정길자의 대를 이은 조선왕조 궁중음식』. Seoul: Institute of Korean Royal Cuisine.
- Hwang, H. S., Han, B. R., Han, B. J. (1989). *Korean Traditional Food*『한국의 전통 음식』. Seoul: Kyomunsa.
- Hwang, H. S., Han, B. R., Han, B. J., Chung, L. (2010). *Three Generations write Korean Traditional Food*『3대가 쓴 한국의 전통음식』. Seoul: Kyomunsa.
- Kang, I. H. (1987). *Taste of Korea*『한국의 맛』. Seoul: Daehantextbook, Co.
- Kim, Y. H., Yang, H. M., Kang, H. K. (2007). *The Very Best of Korean Cooking : Simple Recipes for Beginners*. Seoul: Discovery media.
- Kim, Y. J. (2009). *Korean Cuisine*. Seoul: Yekyong Publishing.
- Korean Food Foundation. (2012). *Great Food, Great Stories From Korea*. Seoul: Korean Food Foundation.
- Korean Food Foundation. (2012). *International Korean Menu Guide*. Seoul: Korean Food Foundation.
- Koreans and Foreigners. (2014). *Korean Food : The Originality, The Impression 2 SET*. Seoul: Dong A Ilbo.
- Labensky, S. R., Hause, A. M. (2003). *Oncooking techniques from expert chefs Third Edition*. Upper Saddle River, NJ: Pearson Education, Inc.
- Lee, A. (2012). *Aeri's Korean Cookbook 1: 100 authentic Korean recipes from the popular Aeri's Kitchen website and YouTube channel*. North Charleston, SC: Createspace Independent Publishing Platform.
- Namkoong, J. (2013). *A Korean Kitchen: Traditional Recipes with an Island Twist*. Honolulu, HI: Mutual Publishing.
- Noh, C. H. (1985). *Practical Korean Cooking*. Elizabeth, NJ: Hollym International corp.
- Park, A. (2007). *Discovering Korean Cuisine: Recipes from the Best Korean Restaurant in Los Angeles*. Torrance, CA: Dream Character.
- Pettid, M. J. (2008). *Korean Cuisine An Illustrated History*. London: Reaktion Books Ltd.
- QA International. (1996). *The Visual Food Encyclopedia: The Definitive Practical Guide to Food and Cooking*. Somerset, NJ: John Wiley & Sons, Inc.
- Samuels, D., Chung, T., Robbins, H. (2008). *The Korean Table: From Barbecue to Bibimbap 100 Easy-To-Prepare Recipes*. North Clarendon, VT: Tuttle Publishing.
- Shin, H. S. Hepinstall. (2001). *Growing up in a Korean Kitchen: A Cookbook*. New York, NY: Ten Speed Press.
- Shugart, G. (1992). *Food for fifty*. New York, NY: Macmillan Publishers Ltd.
- Solomon, C. (2011). *The Complete Asian Cookbook: Japan & Korea*. Richmond, VIC: Hardie Grant Books.
- Song, Y. J. (2011). *The Korean kitchen*. Wigston: Southwater Publishing.
- The Culinary Institute of America. (1996). *The New Professional Chef, Sixth Edition*. New York, NY: Van Nostrand Reinhold.
- Vandenberghe, T., Goossens, J., Thys, L. (2013). *New York Street Food Cooking & Traveling in the 5 Boroughs*. Tielt: Lannoo Publishers.
- Vongerichten, M., Vongerichten, J. G. (2011). *The Kimchi Chronicles: Korean Cooking for an Amerian Kitchen*. Emmaus, PA: Rodale Books.
- Yoo, S, Yoo, J. (2009). *Korean Kitchen*. Seoul: Leescom Publishing.

Index

Anchovies (Dried), about — 22
Janchi-guksu (On-myeon) Noodles in Anchovy Broth — 90
Myeolchi-bokkeum Stir-fried Dried Anchovy — 158
Anchovy Sauce. See Fish Sauce
Anchovy Broth. See Stock
Asian pears. See Pears
Bae. **See Pears**
Baechu. **See Napa Cabbage**
Banchan. **See Side Dishes**
Bap. **See Rice**
Beans, about — 15
Black Beans, about — 15
    Ogok-bap Cooked Five-grain Rice — 78
    Songpyeon Half-moon Rice Cakes — 190
Red Beans, about — 15
    Ogok-bap Cooked Five-grain Rice — 78
    Patjuk Red Bean Porridge — 84
    Songpyeon Half-moon Rice Cakes — 190
Beef, about — 20
Bibimbap Rice Mixed with Vegetables and Beef — 52
Bulgogi Grilled Marinated Beef — 58
Doenjang-jjigae Soybean Paste Stew — 106
Galbi-jjim Braised Short Ribs in Soy Sauce — 60
Gogi-jeon Pan-Fried Beef Cakes — 64
Goldong-myeon (Bibim-guksu) Noodles Mixed with Vegetables and Beef — 92
Gujeol-pan Platter of Nine Delicacies — 138
Japchae Stir-fried Sweet Potato Noodles and Vegetables — 68
Mandu Dumplings — 56
Miyeok-guk Seaweed Soup — 100

Sigeumchi-doenjang-guk Spinach Soybean Paste Soup — 102
So-gogi beoseot-jeongol Beef and Mushroom Hot Pot — 110
Yukgaejang Spicy Beef Soup — 112
Beef Broth. See Stock
Bellflower Roots, about — 18, 33
Doraji-namul Seasoned Bellflower Roots — 166
Black Pepper about — 26
Bibim-naengmyeon Spicy Buckwheat Noodles — 88
Mul-naengmyeon Buckwheat Noodles in Chilled Broth — 86
Samgye-tang Ginseng Chicken Soup — 114
Black Beans. See Beans
Bokkeum. See Stir-frying
Braising
Dak-bokkeum-tang Spicy Braised Chicken — 126
Dak-jjim Braised Chicken in Soy Sauce — 124
Dubu-jorim Braised Dubu in Soy Sauce — 152
Galbi-jjim Braised Short Ribs in Soy Sauce — 60
Gamja-jorim Braised Potatoes in Soy Sauce — 156
Saengseon-jorim Spicy Braised Fish — 148
Bracken, about — 18
Gosari-namul Seasoned Bracken — 166
Carrots, about — 18
Dak-bokkeum-tang Spicy Braised Chicken — 126
Dak-jjim Braised Chicken in Soy Sauce — 124
Galbi-jjim Braised Short Ribs in Soy Sauce — 60
Gimbap Toasted Laver Rolls — 70
Gujeol-pan Platter of Nine Delicacies — 138
Japchae Stir-fried Sweet Potato Noodles and Vegetables — 68
Ojingeo-bokkeum Spicy Stir-fried Squid — 130
So-gogi beoseot-jeongol Beef and Mushroom Hot Pot — 110

Chicken, about — 20

Dak-bokkeum-tang Spicy Braised Chicken — 126

Dak-jjim Braised Chicken in Soy Sauce — 124

Kal-guksu Noodles in Broth — 94

Maekom-dak-gangjeong Deep-fried Chicken with Sweet and Spicy Sauce — 74

Samgye-tang Ginseng Chicken Soup — 114

Chicken Broth. See Stock

Chopsticks, about — 216

Cinnamon

Maejakgwa Twisted Honey Cookies — 194

Sujeonggwa Ginger and Cinnamon Punch — 196

Clams, about — 22

Haemul-pajeon Seafood and Green Onion Pancake — 66

Cookies

Maejakgwa Twisted Honey Cookies — 194

Cucumbers, about — 18

Bibim-naengmyeon Spicy Buckwheat Noodles — 88

Gimbap Toasted Laver Rolls — 70

Goldong-myeon (Bibim-guksu) Noodles Mixed with Vegetables and Beef — 92

Gujeol-pan Platter of Nine Delicacies — 138

Japchae Stir-fried Sweet Potato Noodles and Vegetables — 68

Mul-naengmyeon Buckwheat Noodles in Chilled Broth — 86

Oi-naengguk Chilled Cucumber Soup — 104

Oi-so-bagi Cucumber *Kimchi* — 182

Sangchu-oi-saengchae Lettuce Salad with Cucumber — 160

Daechu (Dried). See Jujube

Dan-hobak. See Squash

Dasima. See Kelp

Desserts

Songpyeon Half-moon Rice Cakes — 190

Hwajeon Flower Rice Cakes — 192

Maejakgwa Twisted Honey Cookies — 194

Sujeonggwa Ginger and Cinnamon Punch — 196

Omija-hwachae Omija Punch — 198

Yuja-hwachae Yuja Punch — 200

Dipping Sauce. See Seasoning

Doenjang. See Soybean Paste

Doraji. See Bellflower Roots

Drinks

Sujeonggwa Ginger and Cinnamon Punch — 196

Omija-hwachae Omija Punch — 198

Yuja-hwachae Yuja Punch — 200

Dubu, about — 30

Doenjang-jjigae Soybean Paste Stew — 106

Kimchi-jjigae Kimchi Stew — 108

Mandu Dumplings — 56

Sundubu-jjigae Spicy Soft Dubu Stew — 54

Dumplings

Mandu Dumplings — 56

Eomuk. See Fish Cakes

Eggs

Beoseot-jeon Pan-Fried Mushrooms — 136

Gyeran-jjim Steamed Eggs — 168

Gyeran-mari Rolled Omelet — 170

Gimbap Toasted Laver Rolls — 70

Haemul-pajeon Seafood and Green Onion Pancake — 66

Kimchi-bokkeum-bap Kimchi Fried Rice — 80

Kimchi-jeon Kimchi Pancake — 134

Maekom-dak-gangjeong Deep-fried Chicken with Sweet and Spicy Sauce — 74

Modum-jeon Assorted Savory Pancakes — 64

Saeu-jeon Pan-fried Shirmps — 136

Sundubu-jjigae Spicy Soft Dubu Stew — 54

Tteokguk Sliced Rice Cake Soup — 96

Egg Garnish, about — 47

Fish, about — 20

Godeungeo-gui Grilled Mackerel — 128

Modum-jeon Assorted Savory Pancakes — 64

Myeolchi-bokkeum Stir-fried Dried Anchovy — 158

Saengseon-gangjang-jorim Glazed Fish in Soy Sauce — 150

Saengseon-jorim Spicy Braised Fish ⋯⋯ 148

Fish Cakes

Tteok-bokki Stir-fried Rice Cakes with Gochu-jang Sauce ⋯ 72

Fish Sauce, about ⋯⋯ 26

Anchovy Sauce, about ⋯⋯ 26

    Baechu-kimchi Whole Cabbage Kimchi ⋯⋯ 174

Flour, Rice. See Rice Flour

Flour, Wheat. See Wheat Flour

*Ganjang***. See Soy Sauce**

Garlic (Whole), about ⋯⋯ 26

Bibim-naengmyeon Spicy Buckwheat Noodles ⋯⋯ 88

Dwaeji-bossam Boiled Pork Wrapped with Napa Cabbage ⋯ 122

Mul-naengmyeon Buckwheat Noodles in Chilled Broth ⋯⋯ 86

Myeolchi-bokkeum Stir-fried Dried Anchovy ⋯⋯ 158

Samgye-tang Ginseng Chicken Soup ⋯⋯ 114

Yukgaejang Spicy Beef Soup ⋯⋯ 112

Garlic (Minced), about ⋯⋯ 26

Marinade

    Bibimbap Rice Mixed with Vegetables and Beef ⋯⋯ 52

    Bulgogi Grilled Marinated Beef ⋯⋯ 58

    Dubu-kimchi *Dubu* with Stir-fried Kimchi ⋯⋯ 154

    Dwaeji-bulgogi (*Jeyuk-bokkeum*) Spicy Stir-fried Pork ⋯ 62

    Galbi-jjim Braised Short Ribs in Soy Sauce ⋯⋯ 60

    Gimbap Toasted Laver Rolls ⋯⋯ 70

    Gujeol-pan Platter of Nine Delicacies ⋯⋯ 138

    Gogi-jeon Pan-Fried Beef Cakes, about *Modum-jeon* Assorted Savory Pancakes ⋯⋯ 64

    Goldong-myeon (*Bibim-guksu*) Noodles Mixed with Vegetables and Beef ⋯⋯ 92

    Japchae Stir-fried Sweet Potato Noodles and Vegetables ⋯⋯ 68

    So-gogi-beoseot-jeongol Beef and Mushroom Hot Pot ⋯⋯ 110

Seasoning for Braising, about ⋯⋯ 45

    Dubu-jorim Braised Dubu in Soy Sauce ⋯⋯ 152

    Saengseon-gangjang-jorim Glazed Fish in Soy Sauce ⋯ 150

Saengseon-jorim Spicy Braised Fish ⋯⋯ 148

Seasoning for Namul, about

    Kong-namul Seasoned Soybean Sprouts ⋯⋯ 164

*Gim***. See Laver**

Ginger (Whole), about ⋯⋯ 26

Baek-kimchi White Kimchi ⋯⋯ 178

Bibim-naengmyeon Spicy Buckwheat Noodles ⋯⋯ 88

Dak-jjim Braised Chicken in Soy Sauce ⋯⋯ 124

Dongchimi Radish Water Kimchi ⋯⋯ 186

Kal-guksu Noodles in Broth ⋯⋯ 184

Nabak-kimchi Water Kimchi ⋯⋯ 184

Saengseon-gangjang-jorim Glazed Fish in Soy Sauce ⋯⋯ 150

Sujeonggwa Ginger and Cinnamon Punch ⋯⋯ 196

Ginger (Minced)

Baechu-kimchi Whole Cabbage Kimchi, about ⋯⋯ 174

Dak-bokkeum-tang Spicy Braised Chicken ⋯⋯ 126

Dwaeji-bossam Boiled Pork Wrapped with Napa Cabbage ⋯ 122

Mat-kimchi (*Seokbakji*) Napa Cabbage and Radish Kimchi ⋯ 180

Oi-so-bagi Cucumber Kimchi ⋯⋯ 182

Ojingeo-bokkeum Spicy Stir-fried Squid ⋯⋯ 130

Saengseon-jorim Spicy Braised Fish ⋯⋯ 148

Ginger (Juice)

Baechu-geot-jeori Fresh Kimchi ⋯⋯ 162

Dwaeji-bulgogi (*Jeyuk-bokkeum*) Spicy Stir-fried Pork ⋯⋯ 62

Maejakgwa Twisted Honey Cookies ⋯⋯ 194

Ginseng, about ⋯⋯ 26

Samgye-tang Ginseng Chicken Soup ⋯⋯ 114

*Gochu***. See Red Chili Pepper**

*Gochu-jang***. See Red Chili Pepper Paste**

*Gochut-garu***. See Red Chili Pepper Powder**

*Gosari***. See Bracken**

Grains, about ⋯⋯ 15

Ogok-bap Cooked Five-grain Rice ⋯⋯ 78

Green onions, about ⋯⋯ 26

Baechu-geot-jeori Fresh Kimchi ⋯⋯ 162

Baechu-kimchi Whole Cabbage Kimchi, about ⋯⋯ 174

Baek-kimchi White Kimchi — 178
Bibimbap Rice Mixed with Vegetables and Beef — 52
Bibim-naengmyeon Spicy Buckwheat Noodles — 88
Bulgogi Grilled Marinated Beef — 58
Dak-bokkeum-tang Spicy Braised Chicken — 126
Dak-jjim Braised Chicken in Soy Sauce — 124
Gyeran-jjim Steamed Eggs — 60
Gyeran-mari Rolled Omelet — 170
Doenjang-jjigae Soybean Paste Stew — 106
Dongchimi Radish Water Kimchi — 186
Dubu-jorim Braised Dubu in Soy Sauce — 152
Dubu-kimchi Dubu with Stir-fried Kimchi — 154
Dwaeji-bossam Boiled Pork Wrapped with Napa Cabbage — 122
Dwaeji-bulgogi (*Jeyuk-bokkeum*) Spicy Stir-fried Pork — 62
Galbi-jjim Braised Short Ribs in Soy Sauce — 60
Godeungeo-gui Grilled Mackerel — 128
Gogi-jeon Pan-Fried Beef Cakes — 64
Goldong-myeon (*Bibim-guksu*) Noodles Mixed with Vegetables and Beef — 92
Gujeol-pan Platter of Nine Delicacies — 138
Haemul-pajeon Seafood and Green Onion Pancake — 66
Japchae Stir-fried Sweet Potato Noodles and Vegetables — 68
Kal-guksu Noodles in Broth — 94
Kimchi-jeon Kimchi Pancake — 134
Kimchi-jjigae Kimchi Stew — 108
Galbi-gui Grilled Beef Short Ribs — 120
Mandu Dumplings — 56
Mat-kimchi (*Seokbakji*) Napa Cabbage and Radish Kimchi — 180
Nabak-kimchi Water Kimchi — 184
Neobiani Grilled Marinated Beef Slices — 118
Nokdu-bindae-tteok Mung Bean Pancake — 132
Oi-naengguk Chilled Cucumber Soup — 104
Oi-so-bagi Cucumber Kimchi — 182
Ojingeo-bokkeum Spicy Stir-fried Squid — 130
Saengseon-gangjang-jorim Glazed Fish in Soy Sauce — 150
Saengseon-jorim Spicy Braised Fish — 148

Samgye-tang Ginseng Chicken Soup — 114
Samsaek-namul Three-Colored Seasoned Vegetables — 164
Sigeumchi-doenjang-guk Spinach Soybean Paste Soup — 102
So-gogi beoseot-jeongol Beef and Mushroom Hot Pot — 110
Sundubu-jjigae Spicy Soft Dubu Stew — 54
Tangpyeong-chae Mung Bean Jelly Mixed with Vegetables — 140
Tteokguk Sliced Rice Cake Soup — 96
Yukgaejang Spicy Beef Soup — 112

Grilling
Bulgogi Grilled Marinated Beef — 58
Godeungeo-gui Grilled Mackerel — 128
Galbi-gui Grilled Beef Short Ribs — 120
Neobiani Grilled Marinated Beef Slices — 118

Gui. See Grilling

Guk. See Soups and Stock

Guksu. See Noodles

Gyeran Jidan (Fried Egg). See Egg

Hobak. See Squash and Zucchini

Honey, about — 26
Songpyeon Half-moon Rice Cakes — 190
Hwajeon Flower Rice Cakes — 192
Maejakgwa Twisted Honey Cookies — 194

Jeon. See Pan-frying

Jeongol. See Stews

Jjigae. See Stews

Jjim. See Braising

Jorim. See Braising

Jujube, about — 19
Baek-kimchi White Kimchi — 178
Galbi-jjim Braised Short Ribs in Soy Sauce — 60
Samgye-tang Ginseng Chicken Soup — 114

Juk. See Porridge

Kelp, about — 23

Kimchi, about — 35
Baechu-kimchi Whole Cabbage Kimchi — 174
Baek-kimchi White Kimchi — 178

Mat-kimchi (*Seokbakji*) Napa Cabbage and Radish Kimchi · 180
Oi-so-bagi Cucumber Kimchi · 182
Water Kimchi
    Dongchimi Radish Water Kimchi · 186
    Nabak-kimchi Water Kimchi · 184
Korean pears. See Pears
Korean Young Squash. See Squash
Laver, about · 22
    Gimbap Toasted Laver Rolls · 70
Lettuce, about · 16
Sangchu-oi-saengchae Lettuce Salad with Cucumber · 160
Makgeolli · 213
***Mandu*. See Dumplings**
***Maneul*. See Garlic**
Marinade. See Seasoning
Meat. See Beef/Pork/Chicken
***Miyeok*. See Seaweed**
***Mu*. See White Radish**
***Muk*. See Mung Bean Jelly**
Mung Bean Sprouts, about · 18
Gujeol-pan Platter of Nine Delicacies · 138
Gungjung-tteok-bokki Royal Stir-fried Rice Cakes · 144
Mandu Dumplings · 56
Nokdu-bindae-tteok Mung Bean Pancake · 132
So-gogi beoseot-jeongol Beef and Mushroom Hot Pot · 110
Tangpyeong-chae Mung Bean Jelly Mixed with Vegetables · 140
Mung Beans, about · 15
Nokdu-bindae-tteok Mung Bean Pancake · 132
Mung Been Jelly, about · 31
Tangpyeong-chae Mung Bean Jelly Mixed with Vegetables · 140
Mushrooms, about · 18
Bulgogi Grilled Marinated Beef · 58
Doenjang-jjigae Soybean Paste Stew · 106
Pyogo (**Shiitake**) **Mushroom, about** · 18
    Beoseot-namul Seasoned Mushrooms · 164
    Bibimbap Rice Mixed with Vegetables and Beef · 52

Galbi-jjim Braised Short Ribs in Soy Sauce · 60
Goldong-myeon (*Bibim-guksu*) Noodles Mixed with Vegetables and Beef · 92
Gujeol-pan Platter of Nine Delicacies · 138
Japchae Stir-fried Sweet Potato Noodles and Vegetables · 68
So-gogi beoseot-jeongol Beef and Mushroom Hot Pot · 110
Oyster Mushroom, about · 18
    Beoseot-jeon Pan-Fried Mushrooms · 136
    So-gogi beoseot-jeongol Beef and Mushroom Hot Pot · 110
    Sundubu-jjigae Spicy Soft Dubu Stew · 54
Mustard, about · 26
Bibim-naengmyeon Spicy Buckwheat Noodles · 88
Gujeol-pan Platter of Nine Delicacies · 138
Mul-naengmyeon Buckwheat Noodles in Chilled Broth · 86
***Myeolchi*. See Anchovies**
***Myeon*. See Noodles**
***Namul*. See Seasoned Vegetables**
Napa Cabbage, about · 16
Baechu-kimchi Whole Cabbage Kimchi · 174
Dubu-kimchi Dubu with Stir-fried Kimchi · 154
Kimchi-bokkeum-bap Kimchi Fried Rice · 80
Kimchi-jeon Kimchi Pancake · 134
Kimchi-jjigae Kimchi Stew · 108
Baek-kimchi White Kimchi · 178
Dwaeji-bossam Boiled Pork Wrapped with Napa Cabbage · 122
Mat-kimchi (*Seokbakji*) Napa Cabbage and Radish Kimchi · 180
Nabak-kimchi Water Kimchi · 184
Noodles, about · 28
Janchi-guksu (*On-myeon*) Noodles in Anchovy Broth · 42
Mul-naengmyeon Buckwheat Noodles in Chilled Broth · 40
Nuts, about · 19
Chestnuts, about · 19
    Baek-kimchi White Kimchi · 178
    Galbi-jjim Braised Short Ribs in Soy Sauce · 60
    Samgye-tang Ginseng Chicken Soup · 114
Pine Nut, about · 19

Maejakgwa Twisted Honey Cookies	194
Sujeonggwa Ginger and Cinnamon Punch	196
Omija-hwachae Omija Punch	198

Peanut, about — 19

Maekom-dak-gangieong Deep-fried Chicken with Sweet and Spicy Sauce — 74

Omija **Berry, about** — 12

Omija-hwachae Omija Punch — 198

Onions

Baechu-geot-jeori Fresh Kimchi	110
Bulgogi Grilled Marinated Beef	58
Dak-bokkeum-tang Spicy Braised Chicken	126
Dak-jjim Braised Chicken in Soy Sauce	124
Dubu-kimchi Dubu with Stir-fried Kimchi	154
Dwaeji-bossam Boiled Pork Wrapped with Napa Cabbage	122
Dwaeji-bulgogi (*Jeyuk-bokkeum*) Spicy Stir-fried Pork	62
Galbi-jjim Braised Short Ribs in Soy Sauce	60
Gungjung-tteok-bokki Royal Stir-fried Rice Cakes	144
Kimchi-jjigae Kimchi Stew	108
Nokdu-bindae-tteok Mung Bean Pancake	132
Ojingeo-bokkeum Spicy Stir-fried Squid	130
Saengseon-gangjang-jorim Glazed Fish in Soy Sauce	150
Saengseon-jorim Spicy Braised Fish	148
Samgye-tang Ginseng Chicken Soup	114
Sigeumchi-doenjang-guk Spinach Soybean Paste Soup	102
Yukgaejang Spicy Beef Soup	112

Oyster Mushroom. See Mushroom

Pa. **See Green onions**

Pancake (Savory)

Haemul-pajeon Seafood and Green Onion Pancake	66
Kimchi-jeon Kimchi Pancake	134
Modum-jeon Assorted Savory Pancakes	64
Nokdu-bindae-tteok Mung Bean Pancake	132
Saeu-jeon Pan-Fried Shirmps	136
Beoseot-jeon Pan-Fried Mushrooms	136

Pan-frying. See Pancake

Peanut. See Nuts

Pears, about — 19

Baechu-kimchi Whole Cabbage Kimchi	174
Baek-kimchi White Kimchi	176
Bibim-naengmyeon Spicy Buckwheat Noodles	88
Bulgogi Grilled Marinated Beef	58
Galbi-jjim Braised Short Ribs in Soy Sauce	60
Mul-naengmyeon Buckwheat Noodles in Chilled Broth	86
Omija-hwachae Omija Punch	198

Peppers. See Red/Green/Black pepper

Perilla Leaves, about — 16

Goldong-myeon (*Bibim-guksu*) Noodles Mixed with Vegetables and Beef — 92

Pine nut. See Nuts

Pork, about — 20

Dwaeji-bossam Boiled Pork Wrapped with Napa Cabbage	122
Dwaeji-bulgogi (*Jeyuk-bokkeum*) Spicy Stir-fried Pork	62
Dubu-kimchi Dubu with Stir-fried Kimchi	154
Kimchi-bokkeum-bap Kimchi Fried Rice	80
Kimchi-jjigae Kimchi Stew	108
Nokdu-bindae-tteok Mung Bean Pancake	132
Sundubu-jjigae Spicy Soft Dubu Stew	54

Porridge

Hobak-juk Pumpkin Porridge	82
Patjuk Red Bean Porridge	84

Potatoes

Dak-bokkeum-tang Spicy Braised Chicken	126
Dak-jjim Braised Chicken in Soy Sauce	124
Doenjang-jjigae Soybean Paste Stew	106
Gamja-jorim Braised Potatoes in Soy Sauce	156
Japchae Stir-fried Sweet Potato Noodles and Vegetables	68

Poultry. See Chicken

Pressure Cooker — 40

Pumpkin. See Squash

Pyogo (**Shiitake**) **Mushroom. See Mushroom**

Radish (White), about — 18

Baechu-kimchi Whole Cabbage Kimchi — 174

Baek-kimchi White Kimchi — 178

Bibim-naengmyeon Spicy Buckwheat Noodles — 88

Dongchimi Radish Water Kimchi — 186

Dwaeji-bossam Boiled Pork Wrapped with Napa Cabbage — 122

Galbi-jjim Braised Short Ribs in Soy Sauce — 60

Mat-kimchi (Seokbakji) Napa Cabbage and Radish Kimchi — 180

Mul-naengmyeon Buckwheat Noodles in Chilled Broth — 86

Nabak-kimchi Water Kimchi — 184

Saengseon-jorim Spicy Braised Fish — 148

Saengseon-gangjang-jorim Glazed Fish in Soy Sauce — 150

Radish (Pickled)

Gimbap Toasted Laver Rolls — 70

Red beans. See Beans

Red Chili Pepper, about — 18

Baek-kimchi White Kimchi — 178

Dak-bokkeum-tang Spicy Braised Chicken — 126

Dongchimi Radish Water Kimchi — 186

Mul-naengmyeon Buckwheat Noodles in Chilled Broth — 86

Myeolchi-bokkeum Stir-fried Dried Anchovy — 158

Nabak-kimchi Water Kimchi — 184

Nokdu-bindae-tteok Mung Bean Pancake — 132

Ojingeo-bokkeum Spicy Stir-fried Squid — 130

Saengseon-jorim Spicy Braised Fish — 148

Tangpyeong-chae Mung Bean Jelly Mixed with Vegetables — 140

Red Chili Pepper Paste, about — 24

Bibimbap Rice Mixed with Vegetables and Beef — 52

Bibim-naengmyeon Spicy Buckwheat Noodles — 88

Dubu-kimchi Dubu with Stir-fried Kimchi — 154

Dwaeji-bulgogi (Jeyuk-bokkeum) Spicy Stir-fried Pork — 62

Maekom-dak-gangjeong Deep-fried Chicken with Sweet and Spicy Sauce — 74

Ojingeo-bokkeum Spicy Stir-fried Squid — 130

Saengseon-jorim Spicy Braised Fish — 148

Tteok-bokki Stir-fried Rice Cakes with Gochu-jang Sauce — 72

Red Chili Pepper Powder, about — 24

Baechu-geot-jeori Fresh Kimchi — 162

Baechu-kimchi Whole Cabbage Kimchi, about — 174

Bibim-naengmyeon Spicy Buckwheat Noodles — 88

Dak-bokkeum-tang Spicy Braised Chicken — 126

Doenjang-jjigae Soybean Paste Stew — 106

Dubu-jorim Braised Dubu in Soy Sauce — 152

Dubu-kimchi Dubu with Stir-fried Kimchi — 154

Dwaeji-bossam Boiled Pork Wrapped with Napa Cabbage — 122

Dwaeji-bulgogi (Jeyuk-bokkeum) Spicy Stir-fried Pork — 62

Haemul-pajeon Seafood and Green Onion Pancake — 66

Kal-guksu Noodles in Broth — 94

Mat-kimchi (Seokbakji) Napa Cabbage and Radish Kimchi — 180

Myeolchi-bokkeum Stir-fried Dried Anchovy — 158

Nabak-kimchi Water Kimchi — 184

Oi-naengguk Chilled Cucumber Soup — 104

Oi-so-bagi Cucumber Kimch — 182

Ojingeo-bokkeum Spicy Stir-fried Squidi — 130

Saengseon-jorim Spicy Braised Fish — 148

Sangchu-oi-saengchae Lettuce Salad with Cucumber — 160

Sundubu-jjigae Spicy Soft Dubu Stew — 54

Yukgaejang Spicy Beef Soup — 112

Rice (Short-grain), about — 14

Bibimbap Rice Mixed with Vegetables and Beef — 52

Gimbap Toasted Laver Rolls — 70

Huin-bap Cooked White Rice — 78

Kimchi-bokkeum-bap Kimchi Fried Rice — 80

Ogok-bap Cooked Five-Grain Rice — 78

Rice (Glutinous), about — 24

Ogok-bap Cooked Five-Grain Rice — 78

Rice cakes, about — 30

Songpyeon Half-moon Rice Cakes — 190

Tteok-bokki Stir-fried Rice Cakes with Gochu-jang Sauce — 72

Tteokguk Sliced Rice Cake Soup — 96

Rice Cookers, about — 40

Rice Flour (Short-grain), about — 30

Patjuk Red Bean Porridge — 84

Songpyeon Half-moon Rice Cakes — 190

Rice Flour (Glutinous), about — 30

Hobak-juk Pumpkin Porridge — 82

Patjuk Red Bean Porridge — 84

Rice Powder. See Rice Flour

Rice Vinegar. See Vinegar

Saenggang. **See Ginger**

Salads. See Seasoned Vegetables

Salt, for cooking, about — 24

Seasoned Vegetables

Baechu-geot-jeori Fresh Kimchi — 162

Doraji-namul Sesoned Bellflower Roots — 166

Gosari-namul Seasoned Bracken — 166

Samsaek-namul Three-colored Seasoned Vegetables — 164

Sangchu-oi-saengchae Lettuce Salad with Cucumber — 160

Seasoning, about — 24

Marinade, about — 43

Bibimbap Rice Mixed with Vegetables and Beef — 52

Bulgogi Grilled Marinated Beef — 58

Dubu-kimchi Dubu with Stir-fried Kimchi — 154

Dwaeji-bulgogi (*Jeyuk-bokkeum*) Spicy Stir-fried Pork — 62

Galbi-jjim Braised Short Ribs in Soy Sauce — 60

Gimbap Toasted Laver Rolls — 70

Gujeol-pan Platter of Nine Delicacies — 138

Gogi-jeon Pan-Fried Beef Cakes, about *Modum-jeon* Assorted Savory Pancakes — 64

Goldong-myeon (*Bibim-guksu*) Noodles Mixed with Vegetables and Beef — 92

Japchae Stir-fried Sweet Potato Noodles and Vegetables — 68

So-gogi beoseot-jeongol Beef and Mushroom Hot Pot — 110

Seasoning for Braising, about — 43

Dak-jjim Braised Chicken in Soy Sauce — 124

Dubu-jorim Braised Dubu in Soy Sauce — 152

Gamja-jorim Braised Potatoes in Soy Sauce — 156

Saengseon-gangjang-jorim Glazed Fish in Soy Sauce — 150

Saengseon-jorim Spicy Braised Fish — 148

Seasoning for Dipping Sauce, about — 46

Cho-ganjang Soy Sauce with Vinegar, about — 46

Beoseot-jeon Pan-Fried Mushrooms — 136

Gujeol-pan Platter of Nine Delicacies — 138

Haemul-pajeon Seafood and Green Onion Pancake — 66

Mandu Dumplings — 56

Modum-jeon Assorted Savory Pancakes — 64

Nokdu-bindae-tteok Mung Bean Pancake — 132

Saeu-jeon Pan-Fried Shirmps — 136

Seasoning for Namul, about — 44

Baechu-geot-jeori Fresh Kimchi — 162

Beoseot-namul Seasoned Mushrooms — 164

Doraji-namul Seasoned Bellflower Roots — 166

Gosari-namul Seasoned Bracken — 166

Kong-namul Seasoned Soybean Sprouts — 164

Sangchu-oi-saengchae Lettuce Salad with Cucumber — 160

Sigeumchi-namul Seasoned Spinach — 164

Seasoning for Braising. See Seasoning

Seasoning for Dipping Sauce. See Seasoning

Seasoning for *Namul*. See Seasoning

Seaweed, about — 22

Miyeok-guk Seaweed Soup — 100

Sesame Oil. See Seasoning

Sesame Seeds (Toasted). See Seasoning

Shell fish. See also Shrimp (Salted)

Shiitake Mushroom. See Mushroom

Shrimp (Fresh), about — 22

Gyeran-jjim Steamed Eggs — 168

Gujeol-pan Platter of Nine Delicacies — 138

Saeu-jeon Pan-Fried Shirmps — 136

Shrimp (Salted), about — 26

Baechu-kimchi Whole Cabbage Kimchi — 174

Mat-kimchi (*Seokbakji*) Napa Cabbage and Radish Kimchi — 180

Side Dishes

Baechu-geot-jeori Fresh Kimchi — 162

Gyeran-jjim Steamed Eggs — 168

Gyeran-mari Rolled Omelet — 170

Dubu-jorim Braised *Dubu* in Soy Sauce — 152

Dubu-kimchi Dubu with Stir-fried Kimchi — 154

Gamja-jorim Braised Potatoes in Soy Sauce — 156

Gosari-namul Seasoned Bracken — 166

Myeolchi-bokkeum Stir-fried Dried Anchovy — 158

Saengseon-gangjang-jorim Glazed Fish in Soy Sauce — 150

Saengseon-jorim Spicy Braised Fish — 148

Samsaek-namul Three-Colored Seasoned Vegetables — 164

Sangchu-oi-saengchae Lettuce Salad with Cucumber — 160

Soju — 214

Soups and Stews

Doenjang-jjigae Soybean Paste Stew — 106

Kimchi-jjigae Kimchi Stew — 108

Miyeok-guk Seaweed Soup — 100

Oi-naengguk Chilled Cucumber Soup — 104

Samgye-tang Ginseng Chicken Soup — 114

Sigeumchi-doenjang-guk Spinach Soybean Paste Soup — 102

So-gogi beoseot-jeongol Beef and Mushroom Hot Pot — 110

Sundubu-jjigae Spicy Soft Dubu Stew — 54

Tteokguk Sliced Rice Cake Soup — 96

Yukgaejang Spicy Beef Soup — 112

Soy Sauce, about — 24

Bulgogi Grilled Marinated Beef — 58

Cho-ganjang Soy Sauce with Vinegar, about — 46

    Beoseot-jeon Pan-Fried Mushrooms — 136

    Gujeol-pan Platter of Nine Delicacies — 138

    Haemul-pajeon Seafood and Green Onion Pancake — 66

    Mandu Dumplings — 56

    Modum-jeon Assorted Savory Pancakes — 64

    Nokdu-bindae-tteok Mung Bean Pancake — 132

    Saeu-jeon Pan-Fried Shirmps — 136

    Sangchu-oi-saengchae Lettuce Salad with Cucumber — 160

Dak-bokkeum-tang Spicy Braised Chicken — 126

Dak-jjim Braised Chicken in Soy Sauce — 124

Dwaeji-bulgogi (*Jeyuk-bokkeum*) Spicy Stir-fried Pork — 62

Galbi-jjim Braised Short Ribs in Soy Sauce — 60

Goldong-myeon (*Bibim-guksu*) Noodles Mixed with Vegetables and Beef — 92

Gujeol-pan Platter of Nine Delicacies — 138

Japchae Stir-fried Sweet Potato Noodles and Vegetables — 68

Kal-guksu Noodles in Broth — 94

Galbi-gui Grilled Beef Short Ribs — 120

Neobiani Grilled Marinated Beef Slices — 118

Ojingeo-bokkeum Spicy Stir-fried Squid — 130

Soy Sauce for Soup, about — 24

Janchi-guksu (*On-myeon*) Noodles in Anchovy Broth — 90

Kimchi-jjigae Kimchi Stew — 108

Miyeok-guk Seaweed Soup — 100

Oi-naengguk Chilled Cucumber Soup — 104

So-gogi-beoseot-jeongol Beef and Mushroom Hot Pot — 110

Sundubu-jjigae Spicy Soft Dubu Stew — 54

Tteokguk Sliced Rice Cake Soup — 96

Yukgaejang Spicy Beef Soup — 112

Soybean Paste, about — 24

Doenjang-jjigae Soybean Paste Stew — 106

Dwaeji-bossam Boiled Pork Wrapped with Napa Cabbage — 122

Sigeumchi-doenjang-guk Spinach Soybean Paste Soup — 102

Soybean Sprout, about — 18

Mandu Dumplings — 56

Nokdu-bindae-tteok Mung Bean Pancake — 132

So-gogi beoseot-jeongol Beef and Mushroom Hot Pot — 110

Spinach, about — 16

Bibimbap Rice Mixed with Vegetables and Beef — 52

Sigeumchi-doenjang-guk Spinach Soybean Paste Soup — 102

Sigeumchi-namul Seasoned Spinach — 164

Squash, about — 16

Dan-hobak, about — 16

    Hobak-juk Pumpkin Porridge — 82

Korean Young Squash, about — 16

    Janchi-guksu (*On-myeon*) Noodles in Anchovy Broth — 90

Zucchini, about — 33

Kal-guksu Noodles in Broth — 94

Squid, about — 22

Haemul-pajeon Seafood and Green Onion Pancake — 66

Ojingeo-bokkeum Spicy Stir-fried Squid — 130

***Ssam*. See Wraps**

***Ssam-jang*, about** — 46

Stews. See Soups and Stews

Stir-frying

Beoseot-namul Seasoned Mushrooms — 164

Dwaeji-bulgogi (*Jeyuk-bokkeum*) Spicy Stir-fried Pork — 62

Japchae Stir-fried Sweet Potato Noodles and Vegetables — 68

Kimchi-bokkeum-bap Kimchi Fried Rice — 80

Myeolchi-bokkeum Stir-fried Dried Anchovy — 158

Ojingeo-bokkeum Spicy Stir-fried Squid — 130

Stock, about — 40

Anchovy Broth, about — 42

  Sigeumchi-doenjang-guk Spinach Soybean Paste Soup — 102

Beef Broth, about — 40

  Galbi-jjim Braised Short Ribs in Soy Sauce — 60

  Mul-naengmyeon Buckwheat Noodles in Chilled Broth — 86

  So-gogi-beoseot-jeongol Beef and Mushroom Hot Pot — 110

  Tteokguk Sliced Rice Cake Soup — 96

  Yukgaejang Spicy Beef Soup — 112

Chicken Broth, about — 42

Kal-guksu Noodles in Broth — 94

Stone Pots, about — 208

Street Food

Gimbap Toasted Laver Roll — 70

Maekom-dak-gangjeong Deep-fried Chicken with Sweet and Spicy Sauce — 74

Tteok-bokki Stir-fried Rice Cakes with Gochu-jang Sauce — 72

***Tang*. See Soups and Stews**

Tofu, See *Dubu* — 30

***Tteok*. See Rice Cakes**

Vegetables, about — 16

Vinegar, about — 24

Bibim-naengmyeon Spicy Buckwheat Noodles — 88

Gimbap Toasted Laver Rolls — 70

Mul-naengmyeon Buckwheat Noodles in Chilled Broth — 86

Cho-ganjang Soy Sauce with Vinegar, about — 42

  Beoseot-jeon Pan-Fried Mushrooms — 136

  Gujeol-pan Platter of Nine Delicacies — 138

  Haemul-pajeon Seafood and Green Onion Pancake — 66

  Mandu Dumplings — 56

  Modum-jeon Assorted Savory Pancakes — 64

  Nokdu-bindae-tteok Mung Bean Pancake — 132

  Saeu-jeon Pan-Fried Shirmps — 136

  Sangchu-oi-saengchae Lettuce Salad with Cucumber — 160

Water Kimchi. See Kimchi

Wheat Flour (All-purpose)

Gujeol-pan Platter of Nine Delicacies — 138

Haemul-pajeon Seafood and Green Onion Pancake — 66

Maekom-dak-gangjeong Deep-fried Chicken with Sweet and Spicy Sauce — 74

Maejakgwa Twisted Honey Cookies — 194

Mandu Dumplings — 56

Modum-jeon Assorted Savory Pancakes — 64

Kimchi-jeon Kimchi Pancake — 134

Wraps, about — 16, 212

***Yuja*, about** — 18

Yuja-hwachae Yuja Punch — 200

Zucchini. See Squash